SELLING ANXIETY

CARYL RIVERS

SELLING ANXIETY

HOW THE
NEWS MEDIA
SCARE WOMEN

UNIVERSITY PRESS OF NEW ENGLAND Hanover and London

Published by University Press of New England,
One Court Street, Lebanon, NH 03766
www.upne.com
© 2007 by University Press of New England
Printed in the United States of America
5 4 3 2 1

Library of Congress Cataloging-in-Publication Data
Rivers, Caryl.
Selling anxiety : how the news media scare women / Caryl Rivers.
    p.   cm.
Includes bibliographical references and index.
ISBN–13: 978–1–58465–615–9 (cloth : alk. paper)
ISBN–10: 1–58465–615–8 (cloth : alk. paper)
    1. Sex discrimination against women—United States.   2. Sex
role in mass media.   I. Title.
HQ1237.5.U6R58 2007
302.23082'0973—dc22   2006038727

University Press of New England is a member of the Green
Press Initiative. The paper used in this book meets their
minimum requirement for recycled paper.

CONTENTS

ACKNOWLEDGMENTS

This book would not have been possible without the help of Dr. Rosalind Chait Barnett, senior scientist at the Women's Studies Research Center at Brandeis University, and my longtime friend and co-author. Roz and I have written four books together on the lives of women, men, and gender issues in society. Her analysis of social science data, and her wisdom, contributed immeasurably to this book.

Also, many thanks to Rita Henley Jensen, editor of the award-winning journalism website Womensenews, for her continued encouragement and friendship.

And last but not least, thanks to my husband, Alan Lupo, for his unwavering support, help, and advice.

INTRODUCTION READ ALL ABOUT IT! WOMEN ARE A MESS!

It's all bad news.

You can't tell women anymore that they can't achieve (except in math). Who'd believe you? But you can tell women that, if they do achieve, they'll be miserable—as will their children. A peculiar duality affects the news media in the first decade of the twenty-first century. The more that women advance in the world of business, academia, medicine, law, economics—the more desperately gloomy the news about women and achievement becomes. As statistics tell us that women are getting more college degrees, more MBAs, more MDs, the more intense becomes the message that this is all a terrible mistake, that only by returning to traditional lives can women find happiness. It's the media's main message to women, and it gets played over and over again, as the news media become more and more a market culture. What were among the most e-mailed stories about women that appeared in the *New York Times* between 2003 and 2006? Stories claiming that men won't marry smart women, that young Ivy League women just want to be housewives, and that the best and the brightest women are creating an "Opt-Out Revolution," leaving their high-powered jobs to return to home and hearth. All of these stories proved to be untrue, based on bad science, but they live on forever in cyberspace, getting repeated over and over again.

This book will focus on the news media, and here I'll highlight some of the trends I now observe after 30-plus years of media watching. To a degree hardly imagined when I first broke into journalism, the new media climate is a marketing climate, and editors need to create "buzz" around stories in a hyper-competitive arena. When I was a young reporter, women were held in such low regard as makers and consumers of news that their concerns were usually relegated to a low-prestige "women's page." Today, one of the most desirable demographics among news customers is affluent women, and stories that create anxiety over women and achievement sell well to that demographic. The news media today sell anxiety to women the way that advertising sells insecurity about their faces, bodies, and sex appeal. Tell women that their children are going to be wrecks if they take their work seriously or that men will reject them if they get a good job, and you'll get their attention fast. Or, tell them that they are out of the new mainstream by not wanting to focus their lives on husbands and family and you'll get "buzz."

Buzz also gets the writers on 24-hour cable, where simple arguments sell much better than complex ones. Slick marketing has replaced clumsy sexist notions about women's proper role, making those ideas more dangerous, since the new messages are more attractively packaged and often wrapped in a veneer of "research," much of which is badly reported, distorted, and misunderstood. To an appalling degree, news stories overhype the findings of a single study that seems to spell bad news for achieving women, or give prime news space to studies that are poorly designed or do not reflect a broader base of research. The result is that readers can come to believe that "science" decrees that day care ruins children or that men don't like smart women.

Astonishingly, here are trend stories that have become "chain reaction" stories, flashing from one media outlet to another:

- Miserable career women who don't have children.
- Miserable career women who have lousy sex.
- Day care kids who become nasty bullies.
- Nannies who kill babies and bad working mothers who hire these nannies.
- Children of divorced mothers who face lifelong problems.
- Women who get too much education and can't get a man.
- Women who get too much education and become infertile.
- Selfish mothers who neglect their children.
- The death of the family (caused by selfish women).
- Girls who get all the attention in schools while boys languish (caused by evil feminist teachers).
- Women who love their jobs so much they spend most of their time there, neglecting their children.
- Women who only want men for their money.
- (White) women who get murdered.
- Women who age (badly).
- Women who can't do math.
- At-home mothers at war with working mothers.
- Scary women who get power.
- Women (all of them) whose brains suit them only for emotion.

- Brides who run away, CEOs (female) who go to jail, first-lady candidates who are too mouthy.

Market forces drive these stories. Today, not only is the news embedded in images created by advertisers to sell products but, increasingly, the news itself is becoming infected with the values, attitudes, and requirements of Infotainment. Why are the majority of images that we see of women those of *young* women? It's not because there are more of them, because the population is rapidly aging. By 2020 there will be more people over 65 than under 15.[1] But only young women are seen as valuable sales images to aim at people under 25, who are seen as those most likely to be influenced by advertising. Older people are thought to have formed brand loyalty, and are thus less desirable targets. Older women are just of no interest to advertisers. Older men are only slightly more so.

Today, newspapers, magazines, and TV outlets are in a bitterly competitive environment—and so they feel they must serve up news that will attract the demographic desired by advertisers. This pressure is felt at all levels of media, even elite media. The *New York Times* "Arts and Leisure" section, for example, featured on the front page of the section a huge color photo of Britney Spears, navel displayed prominently, while Joanne Woodward's photo was much smaller, in black and white, on an inside page. Woodward was directing her husband, Paul Newman, in a revival of the American classic *Our Town*. Twenty-five years, ago, I'd argue, a rock singer whose major appeal was to teenagers would be inside the section with a small picture, while the principals in the theater classic would be the page one photo.

THE INFOTAINMENT CULTURE

Picture, if you will, a scale on which are balanced the lives of real women on one side and infotainment on the other. Which has the most impact on the images of women we see in the news media? There is no contest—infotainment wins, hands down. Look at newsstand magazines, your average newspaper, at network and cable television. Compare the amount of coverage of foreign news with that of popular culture and celebrities. Who wins?

When I first started in the newspaper business, in the 1960s, celebrities were rarely covered in the news pages. Movies were fodder only for the entertainment pages. There was a lively teen pop culture, but you rarely read about Beach Blanket Bingo, Fabian, Gidget, or even Elvis in the news pages. Adult celebrities made the news columns only when their outrageousness turned world class, as with Liz (Taylor) and Dick (Burton). Journalists who covered movie stars and celebrities were considered a lesser breed, hacks who couldn't make it in the real, serious business of journalism. Today, I'd venture that perhaps 60 percent of journalism students want to cover entertainment, fashion, or movies.

The new dominance of infotainment means that certain types of women get enormous coverage *in the news pages*. These are usually young singers, rock stars, and movie stars. For example, over a two-month period at the end of 2002, actress Jennifer Lopez received more than a thousand mentions in major newspapers included in the data base nexis, while Nancy Pelosi, who had recently been named the first woman leader of democrats in the House, received only 454. More astonishing, in this period when foreign policy dominated the headlines and a possible war with Iraq was expected, national security advisor Condoleezza Rice received 432 mentions, far fewer than Jennifer Lopez. In the same period, actress Halle Berry was the subject of 885 stories, and Cameron Diaz was the subject of 300 stories, while Justice Ruth Bader Ginsberg received 42 mentions and senator Dianne Feinstein of California received 101. In late June of 2006, a nexis search found 580 mentions of actress Angelina Jolie and only 405 of Senator Hillary Clinton, the presumptive frontrunner for the democratic nomination for president.

Now, I have no objection to the press covering celebrities. It has always done so, but never before with such intensity. As veteran journalist Pete Hamill puts it, "To qualify as news, celebrities must do something. Not only that, they must do something that is surprising, interesting, or new. If Mr. Big Name throws the former Mrs. Big Name under the Seventh Avenue bus, that is news. Mr. Big Name sitting with friends in a restaurant is not news."[2] One has to ask whether Jennifer Lopez actually did anything new or surprising to get the 1000-plus media mentions, while Ms. Rice was merely dealing with war and peace.

FULL SPEED BACKWARD

I see the coverage of women in the news media over the past 50 years as an arc. We went from the era when a good woman only got her name in the paper when she was born, was married, or died, to a time when feminism was a big story and the First Woman feature was a staple of newspapers and magazines. I had hoped we would proceed from there to a state of normalcy, where women would be covered much as men are, and the archetypes would fade.

That hasn't happened. Instead, we slid rapidly downhill. Ironically, as women themselves quickly moved into successful careers in law, business, the sciences, journalism, professional sports, medicine, etc., media images became more retrograde. The spunky heroines of the "first woman" newspaper stories and the working-girl heroines on TV like Mary Tyler Moore have been replaced by miserable women who whine that they can't get (or keep) a man. (See *Desperate Housewives*). On one episode of *The Bachelor* a stunningly beautiful young brunette sobs that she's a loser when she doesn't get a rose from the man who is supposed to choose a wife from among 25 women. In the 1940s, when relatively few women actually had careers, Roz Russell, Barbara Stanwyck, Bette Davis, and Katharine Hepburn played feisty, attractive career gals in dozens of movies. Now that there are lots of real feisty, attractive career women out there, the media serves up whiny losers. The newspaper features about "first women" achieving in new careers have been replaced by stories about women who can't get pregnant, can't find a man to commit, hate their bodies, are wretched because they are single or divorced, have sexually transmitted diseases, think they are terrible mothers, and on and on.

The situation today is truly alarming. Major studies show that women are vanishing from coverage in the news pages, and that women's voices are less and less frequently being heard on op ed pages, and on "pundit" television shows. *Washington Post* media reporter Howard Kurtz notes, "Most of the officials, lawmakers, experts and political figures who parade their opinions on Sunday morning television have something in common. They don't wear pantyhose."[3] Women represent a meager 14 percent of guests on the five major network shows.[4] Not only that, the gains women made in newsrooms are diminishing. A major study shows that many women editors plan to leave the business (see chapter 6).

THE SPIRAL OF SILENCE

Feminism, one of the major civil rights movements of the twentieth century, has drifted into what researchers call "The Spiral of Silence." This theory contends that "the media tell us what ideas are popular and are gaining strength, and that people clam up when they think their position is weak because they fear social isolation. This leads others to clam up as well, leading to a spiraling of silence concerning that particular position."[5]

The coverage of feminism also neatly dovetails with another theory of the media, that of "news frames" or narratives. Scholars point out that there are many alternate ways to tell a story, and the storyline, or frame, influences readers' perceptions of the story. Feminism has gone through several narratives, to wit:

Amused Scorn

Narrative One: In the early seventies women were supposed to be desirable, piquant, sultry, dutiful, delightful, interesting, maternal, adorable. Now they wanted to be taken seriously? How droll. This led to some rather serious miscalculations. For example, longtime House member and archsegregationist Howard "Judge" Smith of Virginia tried to derail the civil rights act of 1964 by adding language to the bill that made sex, in addition to race, an illegal basis for denying rights to citizens. The idea, of course, was to make the bill seem extreme. It was one of the great ironies of American history, because that language was later used to support major women's rights legislation—which would have made Judge Smith roll over in his grave.

In 1965, women who tried to present a paper on "Women's Liberation" at a meeting of Students for a Democratic Society, the major student protest group of the "New Left."[6] were laughed at and booed. The massive, nationwide marches to celebrate the fiftieth anniversary of women's suffrage in 1970 were treated with amusement by the television networks.[7] Anchorman Howard K. Smith at ABC began his lead-in with this quote from vice president Spiro Agnew: "Three things have been difficult to tame: the ocean, fools and women. We may soon be able to tame the ocean, but fools and women will take a little longer."

My God, They *Do* Want to be Taken Seriously

Narrative Two: They want rights. They want laws. (The National Organization for Women was formed in 1966, the Equal Rights Amendment was introduced into Congress in 1970 and *Ms.* magazine was founded that same year.) The Visigoths are coming (and hairy-legged to boot)! In the seventies, amusement faded, to be replaced by alarm—and accusations that women were undermining God, love, families, civil order, and even the future of the species, since no man would ever cavort with these terrible women. But sex did not vanish, babies got born, life went on.

Capitalism Awakes

Narrative Three: *All these women doing new things. We can sell them stuff.* This was followed by the first everything stories: police chief, astronaut, DA, marathoner, combat pilot, hockey player—the list went on and on. The service academies were opened to women in 1976. As the seventies progressed and morphed into the eighties, new magazines like *Savvy* and *Working Mother* gained circulation, pants suits for the office were in vogue, Jane Fonda played strong women in *The China Syndrome* and *Julia,* and Ellen Goodman won the Pulitzer prize for commentary in 1980, writing often about women's issues. *Our Bodies, Ourselves,* published by a feminist collective in Boston, became a bestseller.

Feminism Is Dead, It's "Family Values" Time

Narrative Four: Jerry Falwell's Moral Majority heralded the rise of the Christian right, often attacking feminism, in the nineties. An infamous *Time* magazine cover illustrated the decline of feminism in "line up" photographs, from Susan B. Anthony to Gloria Steinem and Betty Friedan to Ally McBeal.[8] Rush Limbaugh coined the word Feminazi, which stuck. In fact, I heard one of my students, a bright and very determined career-oriented young woman, tell another student that she was not a "feminazi." One of the great successes of the right has been to demonize feminism for young women. Most know little about the movement that made possible the very lives they lead as bright, educated women taking an active role in all parts of society. They have opportunities that their grandmothers could not have dreamed of, and yet they are disconnected from a vital part of their history, the women's movement.

The truth is that the major tenets of mainstream feminism have been largely absorbed by young women, who now fill more college seats than men, run marathons, join the Army, play contact sports, and seek out good jobs. But most of the media ink is devoted to how "postfeminist" women have rejected the movement. The more disaffected that young women become from the women's movement, the more it is portrayed as a movement of a fringe group of unattractive man-haters, the less advertisers need to worry about the movement's message that women should not hate their bodies and should pay more attention to their brains than their butts and abs. Since young women are the desirable demographic, the less feminist they are, the more they are vulnerable to advertisers who prey on women's insecurities to sell them cosmetics, diet pills, nose jobs, workout tapes, etc. The news media should be a counterweight to advertising, by showing images of women who are accomplished, educated, interesting—even as they age—but as we've seen, movie stars routinely gobble up far more ink than such women.

THE CANARY IN THE MINE

Women are seen as the early warning system of change. Just as coal miners took canaries into mines because, reacting to poisons that humans could not yet detect, the birds would sicken and die, changes in women are seen as harbingers of toxic change. There tends to be great alarm in some quarters when women enter the armed forces, take on new sports, or deviate from old marriage and childbearing patterns.

This is not a new phenomenon. When women were pressing for the vote, the media of the era were fairly hysterical on the subject. It was said that if women left home to enter the polling booth, they would cease to be the angels of the hearth that men so admired, would become coarse and crass and thus incapable of being good mothers, and the family would be destroyed.

Because of this idea that when women change, chaos is at hand, the media frame of many stories about women is one of alarm. And bad news about women gets consistently overplayed. Women are endlessly shown as facing grave risks if they are too "ambitious." Such articles are often based on bad science, but they get huge play and, as a result, flawed data become immortal. It gets repeated over and over again for years, creating what I call The Great Factoid Sinkhole. Junk science, flawed reporting, and "facts" that are simply wrong start out in the leads of news stories where they are at least presented as new ideas, something less than dogma. But such "news" often migrates from the leads of news stories to the "background" paragraphs, where it is presented as undisputed fact. Do you believe that women over 35 can't find husbands, that most kids in day care are bullies, that children of divorce face inevitable misery? None of this is true, but I often see references to such beliefs as "facts" in news stories. The unending drumbeat of bad news leads women to think that the world is much more dangerous and difficult than it actually is, and can make some women timid and fearful—especially about achieving.

If selling anxiety to women is a media winner, almost equally profitable is preying on men's insecurities and fears. Today, men's wages have been stagnant or declining for nearly two decades, globalism and outsourcing have eroded the 30-year jobs of the industrial age, and white males no longer see themselves as dominant in a nation increasingly nonwhite. And, as women gain financial resources, they can be choosier about whom to marry. In their twenties, women more and more often choose education over early marriage.[9]

The news media have been hysterical about the fact that today, there are more women in college classes than men. A perfect illustration of male angst is the *Business Week* cover showing a huge, smiling girl looming over a much smaller boy, whose face is clouded by doubt. "From Kindergarten to Graduate School, Boys Are Now the Second Sex," reads a headline on the contents page.[10]

Until fairly recently, there were no "news frames" reassuring white men that they were dominant and in charge. There was simply no question about that proposition. Increasingly, news narratives seem designed to reassure men that they are still OK, and powerful, and that women can't measure up. Women can't do math, have the wrong genes for leadership, are "hard-wired" for relationships, not for ambition, want to rush away from work to home and hearth, and have rejected feminism. Of course, if all these were true, among the big losers would be white men, whose middle-class lives are increasingly subsidized by women's incomes. Professor Richard Freeman of the National Bureau of Economic Research at Harvard says that the economic boom of the nineties was due, not to male employment, but to the increase in working women, especially those with children.[11]

THE NOSTALGIA TRAP

Nostalgia is another source of the anxiety base of the news media. The American media tend to exaggerate the dangers of the present while understating the perils of the past. So we see the family as being "in decline," marriage as a dying institution, children troubled as never before, unwed pregnancy as a new phenomenon, day care as damaging children, working women as harming their families. The voices of pop psychologists like Dr. Laura combine with right-wing columnists, radio talk show hosts, and political operatives to produce a backlash drumbeat of doom and gloom, and largely blaming women. A Norman Rockwell idea of the past is widely disseminated, and conservative eras such as the fifties or even the nineteenth century are set up as ideal times. In fact, middle-class Victorian women suffered greatly from hysterical illnesses, addiction to morphine, sexual dysfunctions, and depression.[12] Poor women were mercilessly overworked and abused.

The 1950s' family television shows (still running endlessly on cable) depict women as blissful housewives with husbands who are warm, involved fathers. In fact, married women in the fifties had rates of depression and anxiety that were four times as high as those of men, prompting one expert to call marriage a health hazard for women. Men spent very few hours each week with their children, and children experienced their fathers as remote and unconnected to them. The real past often gets overlooked or ignored while a phony past—*The Way We Never Were* (in the words of family historian Stephanie Coontz)—is glamorized.[13]

THE RISE OF THE RIGHT

Though conservatives regularly complain of liberal bias in the media (more about this later), the real phenomenon is the rise of the right in journalistic legitimacy. When I entered journalism school in the 1960s, American conservatism was widely seen as an anachronism. Among republicans, the moderate, modern internationalist wing of the party represented by Dwight Eisenhower trumped the old Bob Taft wing. Eisenhower sent the federal troops into Little Rock to integrate the schools, which was anathema to rock-ribbed conservatives. Republican luminaries were northeastern moderates like senators Jacob Javits, Ed Brooke, and Kenneth Keating and governors like Nelson Rockefeller and Bill Scranton. Social conservatives were more often democrats than republicans, with lawmakers from the "Solid South" supporting Jim Crow and the eternal separation of the races.

So entrenched were liberal ideas as common-sense wisdom in the late sixties that Richard Nixon's domestic agenda was further to the left than Bill Clinton's 30 years later. Nixon supported affirmative action and other special programs for black Americans, called for national health care, backed federal welfare programs, spent liberally on inner city public schools, and signed Title IX mandating equal money for girls in sports.

After the Goldwater debacle of 1964, pundits declared conservatism dead as a doornail. But a surprising thing happened; the corpse not only stirred but got up and ran. Over the next three decades, the evangelizing of America produced a vibrant and powerful religious right, and at the same time, a new breed of conservatives emerged out of elite universities and formed their own think tanks. Following the lead of William Buckley, these neocons were bright, witty, articulate, and more than presentable at cocktail parties or late night Georgetown suppers. They turned out books and op eds and created magazines that were well funded by conservative dollars.

As liberal pundit Michael Lind notes, these charming conservatives "were wrong about everything in a very sprightly way. They were never for racism, only against desegregation; they did not support apartheid, they merely vilified its victims and critics; they were not in favor of dire poverty, they just objected to any and all government programs that might ameliorate it."[14]

And as for women, the neocons liked them—especially those cute blonde miniskirted conservatives who popped up everywhere on TV denouncing feminism. They decreed that women had never really been oppressed—women just liked staying home better than working, and would "cheerfully choose," in the words of George Will,[15] lower-paying, dead-end jobs when they did work.

But the religious right became the real power base of the Republican Party. To get the nomination GOP hopefuls had to endorse the pro-life litmus test and pacify the Bible belt to a degree unprecedented in modern politics.

(One could not imagine Richard Nixon, a secular pro-science president, putting roadblocks in the way of Stem Cell research.) The attack on women's reproductive rights was one of the most undercovered stories of 2003–04, with not only abortion but also contraception under attack. The FDA reversed its own expert panel to deny women over-the counter access to emergency contraception (see chapter 11).

The more powerful conservatives became, the more they were seen as legitimate in the eyes of journalists, the more feminism was delegitimized. A male agent told me and my longtime co-author, Dr. Rosalind Chait Barnett of Brandeis, that as two women writing about feminism (and not denouncing it) we would be immediately suspect. Young women journalists often seem more suspicious of feminists than they do of conservative anti-feminist women—as if the latter simply could not have any agenda and were thus "pure" in a journalistic sense. Too often, feminists get tossed into the same pot with right-wing militias, extreme animal righters, and vegan witches. The rapidly growing power of the right wing in the media accelerates the power of the messages generated by the Canary in the Mine Syndrome, the Nostalgia Trap, and the Death of Feminism narrative. The radio dial has been entirely captured by right-wing ideologues, who see feminism as pure evil. But most insidiously, the idea of the death of feminism has steadily seeped into the mainstream media.

THE DEAD HAND OF MYTH

Despite the gains women have made in the press, ancient myths still color media coverage. Two of the most potent are the Myth of Female Weakness and the Myth of Female Strength. In one, a woman is a sniveling, small-brained, hormone-wracked creature so filled with anxieties and chemical twitches it seems a miracle she can get out of bed in the morning. In the other, she's Wonder Woman and Medusa, all wrapped up in one, able to reduce men to besotted fools or emasculate them with a glance. Women are still "the other," prone to be judged by archetypes about women rather than by individual qualities.

Hillary Clinton, for example, has been portrayed alternately as a strong-willed Amazon or a weak, pathetic, wronged wife. In the pre-Monica days, when Strong Hillary was in vogue, I tracked no fewer than fifty mentions of Hillary that used the word "witch or witchlike." When she moved her office into the west wing, forsaking the first lady's traditional east-wing quarters, it became a major story. You'd have thought Rasputin was moving in. One story compared her to the murderess Glenn Close played in *Fatal Attraction*.

On the other hand, after Monica, she became a weak-willed woman who aided and abetted her husband's bad behavior by her passivity.

Male political figures may be called mean and nasty names, but those words don't usually reflect superstition and dread. Did the press ever call Carter, Reagan, Bush, or Clinton a warlock? Or compare them to movie murderers? Already, we are hearing hints that Condi Rice is a steel-willed careerist who has no personal life. If she opts for a presidential run, those high-heeled boots she wears on her trips abroad may be viewed as instruments for kicking men in the you-know-where.

The myth of female weakness cropped up in press coverage of Elizabeth Dole's presidential campaign (which I'll discuss later in some detail). Dole never got the level of coverage that her status implied she should get—she was the only republican who beat Al Gore head-to-head in early polls. But the news media predicted that she couldn't raise money, exaggerated her personal flaws, and presented her as a neophyte despite the fact that she had been a cabinet member. Cronyism may have been the fatal weakness for Supreme Court nominee Harriet Miers, but the disdain for her accomplishments voiced in the media was palpable. She was also mocked for living with her mother, as if she were a genteel spinster lady out of a Tennessee Williams play.

We might have expected such archetypes to fade in the face of social change, but the new marketing culture of the media has in fact revived them. The news media, which are supposed to hold a mirror up to reality, ironically are becoming *more* rather than less affected by archetypal images.

All the above currents combine to produce a stunning anomaly. Never before have women been so economically productive, so much a part of the social political and economic life of the nation; never before have they had such access to the possibility of achievement—which social science tells us is one of the pillars of well-being. Yet the optimism of the media that once prevailed as the second wave of the women's movement crested has all but disappeared. The news is nearly all bad. If you believed the press, you'd assume that modern women were psychological wrecks, miserable in personal relations, joyless at work while causing great damage to their children, desperate in midlife unless they were housewives, filled with regret if their choices had involved ambition.

Sorry, but this is nonsense. I say this as a modern career woman with two successful grown-up kids, three grandkids, a happy long-term marriage, and with my ambition intact. You couldn't drag me back to a prefeminist era with wild horses. I saw what my mother—a brainy, talented woman—went through in the days when there was no "movement" to support women's ambitions, when a working woman was a disgrace to her middle-class husband, when women couldn't get decent jobs, when abused women shut the doors and put on a lot of rouge, when girls couldn't play sports, and when women couldn't get into law school, med school, or journalism school-except as tokens.

I was there. I was one of the "girls" in the balcony at the National Press Club when women had to cover speeches by political dignitaries from a balcony where they stored the TV equipment. I was told a number of times that despite my journalism degree and a national award, I would not be hired simply because I was a woman. I was kept out of more than one prestigious men's dining establishment—even when I was a working journalist who needed to be there to get a story. (I was part of a group of women who took over the men's dining room at the venerable Boston eatery Loch-Obers. The food was mediocre but it felt *sooo* good to be there.)

As noted earlier, the media no longer tells women—as it told both my mother and me—that we can't achieve. (Except in the fields of math and science.) It's simply too obvious that we can achieve. The new message is that the price of achievement is too high. I'm not sure whether the old or the new message is more crippling. At least with the former, the solution was clear: *Just do it.* Today, it's more subtle: *Poor dears, the price for your accomplishment will be unhappiness, regret, failed marriages, wretched children.*

Why does this message still resonate? Because the idea that it is a woman's job to care for everyone else—even at the expense of her own health and happiness—has deep roots in our history and culture. In the past, when women advocated for their rights, they often had to do so by proclaiming that it was precisely their ability to care for others that gave them moral authority. Julia Ward Howe, anti-slavery crusader and suffragist, wrote, "Woman is the mother of the race, the guardian of its helpless infancy, its earliest teacher, its most zealous champion . . . upon her devolve the details which bless and beautify family life."[16] An echo of these sentiments can to be found in the "essential feminism" movement, which argues that women have an inherent ability to care for others that men lack, and thus women are more moral than men. In *Women's Ways of Knowing: The Development of Self, Voice and Mind* (1986), Mary Belenky and her colleagues write that men value excellence and mastery in intellectual matters and evaluate arguments in terms of logic and evidence. "Women, in contrast, are spiritual, relational, inclusive and credulous."[17] If women's whole being is centered on caring, ambition is unnatural. Aspiring to leadership, they say, violates women's essential nature.

It's not hard to see why women fall prey to scare stories about ambition. One way or another, they have been inhaling them all of their lives.

CHAIN REACTIONS

In this book, I've concentrated on what might be called the "chain reaction" stories—those that jump from front-page newspaper story to magazine cover piece to TV soundbite to the buzz in the blogosphere. One can indeed find balanced, well-reported, nuanced, and positive articles about women in the news media, but these are often stand-alone stories. It's the bad news that races through the media like a California forest fire in September. It's the ideas in such stories that have staying power, thanks to sheer repetition. We all read or hear them, one way or another.

Because the media have so much power in our society—more, some say, than the church, the community, the political party or even the family—they can no longer be regarded as mere mass entertainment. Selling anxiety to women can have real consequences for real women's lives. It can dim their dreams, hobble their ambitions, and blunt their courage.

It is to the prevention of such sorry outcomes that this book is devoted.

1
SUPERWOMEN AND TWITCHING WRECKS

Working women in the news media come in two basic styles: Superwomen and Twitching Wrecks.

The former are often profiled in business pages, lifestyle pages, and TV features. They are accomplished, incredibly organized, and never seem to sweat. Since I've written a number of books, I have been the subject of such stories, and I rarely recognize the dynamo presented on the pages. It's what they *don't* report that intrigues me.

They do not say, for example, that there are so many dust kitties in my house that I am considering applying to the Department of Agriculture for a subsidy to raise them. I never even owned an iron until my kids were in their late teens. They wore stuff just the way it came out of the dryer. I never wrote thank you notes—or any kind of notes. My son forged his own "please excuse Steven's absence, he had the flu" notes to take to the principal. If you are my friend and you die, don't expect your heirs to hear from me. It's not that I don't care—I'm too busy and too disorganized to deal with it. The whole thrust of the Superwoman genre of story appears to present women who are so, well, super, in their entire lives that no ordinary woman can possibly hope to emulate them. On the surface such stories seem as if they are presenting role models, but the fact is they are presenting the very antithesis—women so far above the madding crowd that they intimidate rather than encourage.

On the other end of the media spectrum are the Twitching Wretches. They seem to inhabit every "working woman" trend story that rolls off the presses or onto videotape. Such women are endlessly miserable, eternally frazzled. Here's *US News and World Report:* "The first time Kristen Garris, 29, dropped off her 10-week-old daughter, Bailey, at the day care center, she says, "I cried the whole way to work."[1]

And *Newsweek:*[2] "For the New York lawyer, it all hit home in the grocery store. She had stopped in with her six-year-old to pick up a few things. But since the babysitter normally did the shopping, she was unprepared for what was about to happen. Suddenly, there was her son, whooping and tearing around the store, skidding the length of the aisles on his knees. *This can't be my son* she thought in horror. Then the cashier gave a final twist of the knife. 'Oh,' she remarked, 'So you're the mother!'" The upshot? The mother leaves her good job to work part-time in a suburb. One does wonder, however, why she was so upset. Any mother of a six-year-old has seen the kid go wild in supermarket aisles. It's in their genes. I would, in fact, *worry* about a child so well behaved that he or she was able to resist using the aisles as a running track or grabbing produce from the shelves.

From my database surveys, the "twitching wrecks" news frame in the media far outnumber happy, competent women who like their jobs and manage well, except in specialized publications like *Working Mother*. Women are miserable at work, say the media, in such stories as these:

- The Majority of Working Women Are Stressed Out (UPI).[3]
- Female Managers Face Super Stress (*Chicago Tribune*).[4]
- Working Women Stressed Out (Reuters).[5]
- Life's a Nightmare for Today's Middle-Class Working Mothers (*Guardian*).[6]
- *Business Week* declared a blues epidemic among working women.[7]
- Are You Headed for Overload? (*Redbook*).[8]

You would think that something—or someone—was forcing all those miserable women to stay at their jobs, instead of running home where they would really be happy. But what does reliable social science research say? Dr. Rosalind Barnett and I examined the data in our book *She Works, He Works*.[9] Nearly two decades of well-designed, reliable research find working women consistently healthy—healthier, in fact, than homemakers. A national longitudinal study[10] analyzed at the University of Michigan found women who combined work and family had better physical health and fewer emotional problems than homemakers. A federally funded three-year study found working women emotionally healthier than those not employed.[11] According to a 22-year-long UC Berkeley study, at age 43, homemakers had more chronic conditions and were more disillusioned and frustrated than employed women.[12] The Framingham heart study finds no heart problems in most working women—it's only those in dead-end jobs with low pay, repetitive tasks, and little control over working conditions who have problems.[13] (It's a lousy job that offers high demand and low control that can literally be a killer, the study says, especially if you have little help at home. Many women have such jobs.) One major study found that having a baby did not increase psychological distress for a woman—*unless she dropped out of the workplace!*[14] A 2005 study of 1,053 mothers found that children of working mothers do not suffer socially or intellectually if their mothers work outside the home.[15]

A veritable Everest of research tells us that, on the whole, real women are doing well at work, facing stress but handling it well, especially if they have well-paid and challenging jobs. But in the media, the Twitching Wrecks are the story, especially the ones who give up and go home. After the *Boston Globe* ran a profile of an anchorwoman who had left her job, Associate Professor Jeff Melnick of Babson College wrote, in a letter to the editor, "So what's with the working mother guilt trip? I'm wondering if anyone at the *Globe* has noticed how many times in the past five years or so you have run approving Living/Arts features about mothers who have renounced the 'fast track' in order to stay home with their kids. The one about the TV news anchor was only the latest in what seems like an onslaught of 'backlash' pieces about the impossibility of balancing work life and home life."[16]

And it's usually stories about lawyers, brokers, managers, and other prestige workers that are featured in the newspapers and magazines, because that's who the desired readers are. Too little newsprint is wasted on the poor and working-class women who face the real problems at work that cause severe health risks. (See Barbara Ehrenreich's *Nickel and Dimed: On (Not) Getting By in America,* 2001.[17]) As a society, we are insisting that welfare mothers march off to jobs that are high-stress and low-paid, while their kids are either home alone or in the care of a neighbor. At exactly the same time, the media are lecturing women with good jobs and excellent child care that they are at risk for stress and are probably rotten mommies to boot. Does this make sense?

But no matter. The news media still insist that going home is what all women really want to do. I've followed several of the women-going-home news trendlets over the years, and you can almost hear the sigh of relief behind them. *Well, now they're doing it. Finally they are going home. (Where, of course we always knew they belonged.)*

But nearly all the trends are phony. In the early nineties, misreading of census data led to a whole spate of such stories, with headlines like these:

- More Supermoms Are Hanging Up Their Capes (*Orlando Sentinel*).[18]
- Is Superwoman Shedding Her Cape? (*Atlanta Constitution*).[19]
- The Failed Superwoman (*Ebony*).[20]
- Superwoman Has Had Enough (*The Independent*).[21]

What led to all this? A slight dip in the number of women in the workforce. But, in fact, the dip among *men* entering the workforce was greater than that of women. Were men going home to bake cookies, shedding their superheroes' capes, just longing for home and hearth? Hardly. Most likely, it was the sluggish economy at the time that led to the dip. Had the news media put the statistics in context, those stories would have fallen apart.

This "bad news" narrative, however, proved hard to dismiss. The *New York Times* highlighted it in a 2002 feature on female executives who had left their high-level jobs.[22] "They Conquered, They Left," announced the *Times,* and in a large black subhead added, "Some say women have less psychic investment in careers." When Jane Swift stepped down as Governor of Massachusetts, Rosie O'Donnell left her talk show, and presidential aide Karen Hughes left the White House to go back to Texas, the news media used these particular women as archetypes for *all* women. The media almost never use individual men as archetypes for an entire gender, as they do with women. These kinds of stories never appear when powerful men leave jobs. When labor secretary Robert Reich quit the Clinton cabinet, saying he wanted to spend more time with his kids, there was no story about "men" leaving. No stories surfaced when senators Fred Thompson and Phil Gramm said they were calling it quits. But men do leave, of course. Jane Swift's old boss, Paul Cellucci, left the Massachusetts governor's job to take an ambassador's spot, a job with much less power and visibility. He is just one of a long list of such men. Men, in fact, leave good jobs all the time for a variety of reasons, including family, but you never read much about this, because it's not seen as a "trend."

But the women-going-home trend story rolls relentlessly on. *Time* magazine wrote of a "reluctant revolt" of mothers who are going home and the *New York Times Magazine* sounded this same theme in one of its most controversial cover articles, 2003's "The Opt-Out Revolution."[23] (The cover illustration shows a young woman with a toddler on her lap, sitting in front of a ladder.) The sweeping nature of the title and the placement of the article on the cover implies that the author, Lisa Belkin, is examining a pervasive national trend. "Many high-powered women today don't ever hit the glass ceiling, choosing to leave the workplace for motherhood. Is this the failure of one movement or the beginning of another?" asks the magazine.

Here is an example, all too common in today's news media, of the over-hyping of a story to make it seem more important than it really is. This major article is based on no systematic research; rather it is a collection of anecdotes from a very nonrepresentative sample. Belkin based nearly her entire story on small groups of Princeton graduates who were members of book groups in several cities and who had husbands affluent enough to finance a comfortable lifestyle on one income. And even though these women were presented as opting out "by choice," that's not quite an accurate picture. One television news reporter, for example, had asked her station for a part-time contract, but was refused. They said it was all or nothing, so she left—and called it a wrenching decision. "It kills me that I'm not contributing to my 401(k) anymore," she said. Another woman, a lawyer, decided to leave her firm only after a judge made an arbitrary schedule change on a major case on which she had been working intensely for months—while nursing her daughter. The schedule change made her life nearly impossible.

Do these women in fact constitute a revolution? Are they even typical of their Princeton classes? We have no idea, because Belkin gives us little data. Are these women really "opting out?" One woman Belkin quotes says, "It's not black or white, it's gray. You're working. Then you're not working. Then you're working part time or consulting. Then you go back. This is a chapter, not the whole book." Another says, "I'm doing what is right for me at the moment. Not necessarily what is right for me forever." The author herself writes that all the professional women she has spoken to who made the choice to stay home say they have made a temporary decision for just a few years, not a permanent decision for the rest of their lives. They have not lost their skills, just put them on hold.

And one woman notes that, "The exodus of professional women from the workplace isn't really about motherhood at all. It is really about work." She adds, "There's a misconception that it's mostly a pull toward motherhood and her precious baby that drives a woman to quit her job . . . not that the precious baby doesn't magnetize many of us. Mine certainly did. As often as not, though, a woman would have loved to have maintained some version of a career, but that job wasn't cutting it anymore. Among women I know, quitting is driven as much from the job dissatisfaction side as from the pull to motherhood."

This would have been an interesting article about some educated women making individual career decisions if it hadn't been incredibly overplayed. Why did it need an exaggerated title, a cover graphic that shows a woman holding a baby with the abandoned career ladder in the background, and the simplistic headline suggesting that this issue is only about women "choosing" to leave work? The article's tagline also suggests, hyperbolically, that this may be a "failure" of feminism (though, later on, the author herself contradicts that idea.) In fact, wasn't feminism all about giving women more choices? Most important, what the article really shows is the inflexibility of the workplace. Many of these women didn't opt out. They in fact wanted to keep working, but were presented with impossible choices—either working insanely long hours or not working at all.

The Belkin article suggests that professional and management-level women are focusing more on home and hearth and abandoning serious careers. Is this in fact true? Does such a major trend really exist? No. Citing the *Times* article, sociologist Kathleen Gerson of NYU notes, "the media start their annual claim that the new generation of women is turning away from careers to care for their families."[24] This idea, Gerson says, is nonsense. "Over the past 30 years, reversing previous historical trends, highly educated, well-employed women have become more likely to marry and have a child than their counterparts with fewer educational credentials, even though they tend to start families later. Educated women are especially likely to be in the work force. A 2001 census survey of all mothers with children under six found that 68 percent of women with college degrees and 75 percent of women with postgraduate degrees are in the labor force. They are three times as likely to work full time as part time." In 2006, economist Heather Boushy analyzed the most recent data and wrote, "Contrary to conventional wisdom, highly educated mothers are MORE likely to be in the labor force than women with less education or less demanding careers . . . Between 2000 and 2004, the labor force participation by mothers did go down—but so did the labor force participation of childless women and of men. In the recession of 2002 to 2005, mothers were not opting out of employment—they were simply not finding jobs. In the long run, the trend is for mothers to opt in when they can find jobs!"[25]

There's the truth. Women do not regularly opt out of demanding management jobs for home and hearth. And since the Labor Department reports that about 45 percent of all managerial posts are held by females, the tide of women running home must indeed be a trickle.[26]

One major study of high-level women failed to uncover an "Opt-Out" trend. Linda Stroh, Jeanne Brett, and Anne Reilly of Loyola studied 1,029 men and women managers who not only had the same level of jobs, but also the same levels of education and time in the workforce, and who had relocated for their careers.[27] Not only did these women *not* opt out of demanding jobs, they were as devoted to their jobs as the men were to theirs. When they left, it wasn't to go home, it was for the same reason men left: better jobs and more advancement. Since women in corporations are more likely to stall out at lower levels than men, it's no surprise that more of them get frustrated and leave. Many form their own businesses, where they won't run into glass walls and ceilings. Stroh, Brett, and Reilly say that this defection is not due to qualities women managers lack, or to anything they are doing wrong, but to persistent discrimination.

One female investment professional told the *New York Times* that she believed she was denied a promotion because she was a woman, but decided not to waste time trying to figure it out. Instead, she simply joined another firm.[28] And Janet Tiebout Hanson, who spent fourteen years at Goldman Sachs, asked, "Why spend ten or fifteen years hitting the glass ceiling? Why not go directly to Go and collect $200?" She left Goldman and founded her own investment firm, Milestone Capital Management.[29] Stroh, Brett, and Reilly say, flatly, "Corporate America has run out of explanations that attribute women's career patterns to women's own behavior. It is time for corporations to take a closer look at their own behavior."

Well, the fact is that every day thousands of women in important, well-paid jobs do not leave them. Thousands of women do their work, perform more than competently, and relate well to their kids. But that's rarely news. The women who stay in good jobs and do well are the huge majority—those who leave are in a small minority. It's the same old story as the "Superwoman Is Leaving" headlines of the nineties. A temporary weak labor market creates a slight downtick in the steady, upward march of women into the workplace and the media rush in with yet another fake trend.

When women do leave jobs, news stories imply that these women are returning to domesticity. But will we find then planting peonies in their back gardens? Hardly. Like accomplished men, they will go on to to other achievements. Karen Hughes is back in DC, advising George W., her old boss. Rosie O'Donnell took the TV job in the first place for family reasons—she didn't have to travel the way she did playing the comedy clubs. She's now back on the popular ABC show *The View*. As for Jane Swift, she's the breadwinner in her family, so moved easily into the private sector. She stepped down because her polls were lousy and the state republicans were looking for a white knight—and found one in Mitt Romney. If Swift had wanted to depart for domestic reasons, she would have done so when she had twins while in office. If Mitt hadn't come riding through on his charger, grabbing up the republican big bucks, the political story in Massachusetts would have been "See Jane Run." But the news stories usually use the loaded words "going home," as if the women were about to put on their pearls and start vacuuming like June Cleaver on the old TV sitcom.

A corollary to the "going home" story" popped up in 2005 when a front page story in the *New York Times* reported "Many Women at Elite Colleges Set Career Path to Motherhood."[30] The article, by Louise Story, claimed to have found—through interviews and an e-mailed questionnaire—that 60 percent of women in two Yale dorms planned to jettison career plans in favor of being longtime at-home mothers.

As it turned out, the story was rather thin gruel. It was not written by a *Times* reporter, but by a Columbia journalism student doing her thesis for professor Sylvia Nasar. Critics immediately pounced. Slate media writer Jack Shafer found the "facts" in the story so flimsy that he said the reporter "deserves a week in the stockades. And her editor deserves a month."[31] He pointed out that the writer used the word "many" 12 times, in place of statistics. The e-mail survey she sent around hardly qualified as anything but anecdotal evidence, and it seems the writer edited out those people who didn't fit her thesis, or misrepresented those who appeared to fit. Writing in *The Nation* ("Desperate Housewives of the Ivy League"), Katha Pollitt said she had contacted a number of people at Yale, including professors and students who were interviewed, and "I didn't find one person who felt Story fairly represented women at Yale."[32] Many students said they'd thrown away Story's questionnaire in disgust. Physics professor Megan Urry polled the 45 female students in her class and only two said they planned to stay at home as the primary parent.

The *Times*, it seems, is addicted to the story of women going home—which it runs over and over. Shafer asks, "Is there a *New York Times* conspiracy afoot to drive feminists crazy and persuade young women that their place is in the home?" The real story about young women—which the writer could have told instead of straining to manufacture a fake trend—is that females at elite colleges want good jobs with reasonable hours, so that they can have adequate time with their families. (Men aged 20 to 39 said exactly the same thing in a survey by the Radcliff Public Policy Institute in 2000. Eighty-two percent put family first and 71 percent would sacrifice pay for family time.)[33] But that nuanced, contextual story would not have had much "buzz." It certainly would not have appeared on the front page of the *Times*. While the article was a journalistic failure, in the buzz department it was a big hit. It was the most e-mailed story on the paper's website in its time period. And that was why it was published.

Unfortunately, the paper is missing the real news because of what Pollitt calls its "obsessive focus on the most privileged as bellwethers of American womanhood." What may be truly surprising in the working woman saga is who really is at home. Education is playing a significant role in determining which mothers work and which don't. Among college-educated women, 68 percent of those who had a baby within the last year were employed, compared with only 38 percent of those who had not graduated from high school.[34] But the high-school-grad working mothers are not the desired demographic of elite publications and get little attention. This picture is almost exactly the opposite of the idea that has been popular in the media for years—that women wanted to stay home, and if they had the resources to do so, they would. The women who stayed in the workforce were supposed to be those with the least economic resources who *had* to work.

Demographic projections show that women are living very long lives, and will continue to do so. A 65-year-old woman today can expect to live, on average, 19 more years. An 85-year-old-woman can, on average, expect to live six-and-a-half more years. Some estimate that a white baby girl born today has a good chance of living for a century.[35]

All this raises the very real specter of a legion of older women facing dwindling resources. Those least educated and out of the work force for a significant period of time will be the most vulnerable. They will probably outlive their husbands—and their husbands' pension benefits. And even if they do have some retirement benefits of their own, those may be meager. The Heinz Foundation notes that women retirees receive only half the average pension benefits that men receive and that women's earnings average $.74 for every $1 earned by men—a lifetime loss of over $250,000.[36]

But that's not a sexy media story, and it gets little attention. What this all means is that we have to get the message out to young girls—especially those in poor and working-class families—that staying in school and getting as much education as possible is critical to their future well-being. Our idea that the typical at-home mom is the contented spouse of a high-earning male, baking cookies, lunching with friends, having time to drive her kids around the suburbs, is out of date.

The true picture may be of a woman living close to the economic edge—and very much at risk.

2
TOO TIRED FOR SEX, TOO LATE FOR BABIES?

The continuing backlash against feminism is an amazing phenomenon, like those "shape shifters" that slither about on *Star Trek* and can take more forms than you can manage to count.

One incarnation that absolutely intrigues the media is the idea that working women, especially high-achieving women, have lousy sex. If women do achieve—outside of low-level "pink-collar" jobs—they will be miserable. No man will want them. It's become a recurring theme for the news media.

This idea proved irresistible in the winter of 2005. Citing a pair of studies, the *Chicago Sun Times* headlined "They're Too Smart for These Guys,"[1] *The Toronto Star* asked "Are Men Insecure or Are They Merely Intimidated?"[2] and the *New York Times* proclaimed there were "Glass Ceilings at Altar as Well as Boardroom."[3] Columnist Maureen Dowd chimed in, "Men Just Want Mommy," asking whether the feminist movement was "some sort of cruel hoax." She wrote, "The more women achieve, the less desirable they are."[4]

Dowd, in fact, elaborated on the theme of *smart women are miserable* in a controversial article in the *Times* magazine in the fall of 2005, *"What's a Modern Girl to Do?*[5] She wrote, "the aroma of male power is an aphrodisiac for women, but the perfume of female power is a turnoff for men. It took women a few decades to realize that everything they were doing to advance themselves in the boardroom could be sabotaging their chances in the bedroom."

It's too bad that Dowd—capable of such wit, charm, and political insight in many of her columns—did not bother to check her social science data. She would have discovered that nearly all the "research" she cites in the article had been thoroughly trashed by scientists, was based on flimsy single studies, or was contradicted by much better data.

The findings of the first study Dowd and others cited, by psychologists Stephanie Brown of the University of Michigan and Brian Lewis of UCLA, were hardly the basis of a story about all men.[6] It was done on a tiny sample (120 male and 208 female undergraduates, mainly freshmen). The males rated the desirability of a fictitious female, who was described as either their immediate supervisor, a peer, or an assistant, as a dating or marriage partner.

Surprise, surprise! The freshman males preferred the subordinate over the peer and over the supervisor when it came to dating and mating. But was the study a barometer of *adult* male preferences—or of teenage boys' ambivalence about strong women? Clearly the latter, given the facts about what adult men actually do. Men do not reject achieving women. Quite the opposite. Sociologist Valerie Oppenheimer of UC Berkeley reports that today men are choosing as mates women who have completed their education.[7] The more education a woman has, the more marriageable she is. And Heather Boushey of the Center for Economic Policy Research found that women between the ages of 28 and 35 who work full time and earn more than $55,000 per year or have a graduate or professional degree are just as likely to be successfully married as other working women.[8] Another indicator of the fact that men don't reject ambitious women is that some 40 percent of college-educated women earn more than their husbands, but their marriages are no less stable than those of women whose husbands earn more than they do.[9]

Another major problem with the college males study was that the investigators claimed men's mate preferences have an evolutionary basis; namely, that men's drive to reproduce their genes lead them to prefer relatively subordinate, docile females. Assertive women would be likely to roam, leaving their male partners uncertain about whether any children such women might bear would really be theirs. This same evolutionary theory claims that women seek as mates older, more powerful men who control resources. Women, especially mothers, according to evolutionary psychology, are vulnerable and need the protection that such men can provide. Yet, awkwardly for this theory, the women in the study showed no preference for dominant males over other males for either dating or mating. In fact, the idea that women are "hardwired" to seek out older, rich men has been skewered by recent research. A major review of mate selection data shows that in societies where women have access to resources, they do not choose older "provider" males to marry. Instead, they seek out men who are kind, intelligent and can bond with children, report psychologists Alice Eagly of Northwestern and Wendy Wood of Duke.[10]

All of this information was available to reporters, if they had simply contacted any one of a number of researchers who could have offered a counterpoint to the study featured in the news reports. Rarely was this done.

The second study that fueled the news stories about miserable women was conducted by investigators at four British universities (Edinburgh, Glasgow, Bristol, and Aberdeen).[11] It found that, for every 15-point increase in IQ score above the average, women's likelihood of marrying fell by almost 60 percent. *Atlantic* headlined, in its April 2005 issue, "Too Smart to Marry?"[12] And Dowd told her readers, "a high I.Q. hampers a woman's chance to marry, while it is a plus for men.[13] Really bad news for bright women, right?

Actually, no. What most stories about this study—including Dowd's and the one in the *Atlantic*—failed to mention is that the data were gathered from men and women born in 1921; the women are all now in their eighties. They came of age in a time when the strictures of marriage might well have been unattractive for bright women. In many cases, such women could not even have been employed if they chose to marry. Many schools, for example, would not employ married women with children as teachers as late as the 1960s. In the 1950s, middle-class men whose wives worked were often regarded as failures who were not "good providers." But today, as the statistics cited earlier reveal, men are not rejecting brainy women with good income potential—quite the opposite. This study tells us absolutely zero about the behavior of today's young men and women. Yet, it became part of the fabric of "alarming news" about women with no warning to readers that the data were half a century old.

In her article, Dowd laments the spate of Hollywood movies in which men fall in love with their maids, rejecting women who are more ambitious. In the movie *Spanglish,* she notes, Adam Sandler falls for his beautiful Mexican maid. The maid, "who cleans up for him without being able to speak English, is presented as the ideal woman, in looks and character. His wife, played by Tea Leoni, is repellent: a jangly, yakking, overachieving, overexercised, unfaithful, shallow she-monster." Alas, worries Dowd, "Art is imitating life, turning women who seek equality into selfish narcissists and objects of rejection rather than of affection."

She adds, "It's funny. I come from a family of Irish domestics—statuesque, 6-foot-tall women who cooked, kept house, and acted as nannies for some of America's first families. I was always so proud of achieving more—succeeding in a high-powered career that would have been closed to my great-aunts. How odd, then, to find out now that being a maid would have enhanced my chances with men."

But of course, only in Hollywood fantasy do powerful men marry their maids. "Art" isn't imitating life—just other bad movies. While some males are indeed so threatened that they can't tolerate ambition and achievement in a woman, the data tell us that most men are not looking for doormats to marry.

But the refrain lingers. The 2005 "misery" stories were, in fact, a variation on the same theme that inspired similar headlines in the mid-1980s. As an infamous *Newsweek* magazine cover story put it, women over 40 have as much chance of getting killed by a terrorist as they do of getting married.[14] This story and the many others like it are a prime example of how a major "trend" can grow from the barest of seedlings. Three Harvard–Yale researchers published a study on "Marriage Patterns in the United States," which seemed to justify the "terrorist-marriage" comparison. "Are These Women Old Maids?" screeched *People* magazine, in a headline over pictures of Diane Sawyer, Sharon Gless, Donna Mills, and Linda Ronstadt.[15] "A Harvard–Yale study says that most single women over 35 can forget about marriage," warned the magazine.

Before long, there was hardly a female in the nation who hadn't heard the dire predictions about women who hold off on marriage. The *Newsweek* cover featured an illustration showing how the marriage chances of women allegedly dropped faster than an Olympic downhill skier.[16] The story entered pop culture immortality through one of Nora Ephron's single women in *Sleepless in Seattle* who cited the "killed by a terrorist" line.

But was it true? No. The researchers themselves said their work was being wildly misinterpreted. They had looked at census data on baby boomers, in the light of an established trend for women to marry men who are two to three years older and who are at least as well educated. During the baby boom years, each year brought an increasing number of babies; so the baby crop in 1955 was larger than that in 1953, for example. In the world of statistics, a woman born in 1955 would be looking for a husband among the smaller group of men born in 1953—fishing in waters that contain fewer men.

But the man shortage was only an "older man shortage." The thirty-five-year-old woman who insisted that she would marry *only* a man two years her senior who is as educated or more educated than she could face a shortage. Viewed in this limited statistical prism, the white, college-educated woman's likelihood of marrying was only one in 20. But of course, that number is completely bogus. Why should we assume that this woman would scorn a man her own age? Or the 34-year-old man. Or the 28-year-old man? This is a cover story? No. It's an example of a narrow statistical study, with little relation to how men and women behave in real life, being hyped into a phony "trend."

Newsweek admitted as much 20 years later, on a surprising cover in June of 2006 that announced, "We Were Wrong,"[17] saying that, in fact, no dire consequences had emerged for women who decided to delay marriage. In fact, some 90 percent of the women who were supposed to be forever single had married or would do so.

The way in which the original story was jerrybuilt offers a good example of the construction of media trends. One reason an obscure demographic study acquired such long "legs" as a news story, *Newsweek* admitted, is that the magazine came up with that catchy "terrorist" line, which was not in the academic study.

The line was first written as a joke in a memo from correspondent Pamela Abramson. "It's true; I am responsible for the single most irresponsible line in the history of journalism, all meant in jest," Abramson told *Newsweek* in 2006.

Staff writer Eloise Salholz inserted the clever line into the story, which passed muster with editors, who thought readers would take it as hyperbole. They didn't. As *Newsweek* admits, "Most readers missed the joke." All those mid-eighties gloom-and-doom pieces became building blocks of a monumental cultural commitment to the patently false idea that ambition makes women unhappy and unloved.

But the idea that, for women, good sex and achievement are incompatible is still a riff that the media simply cannot resist. It echoes through the story of Kate Reddy, the heroine of *I Don't Know How She Does It,* the best-selling 2002 novel by British author Allison Pearson.[18] Kate is a high-powered bond trader in England. We meet her when she's trying to "distress" a pair of mince pies so they will look homemade for her daughter's school. Kate's a wreck, trying to do it all. In the end, Kate's husband threatens to leave her for another woman and so she gives up her job and runs home to hubby where she has great sex and happily bakes cookies for her kids.

This book is supposed to speak to all modern women. At least the news media thought so. *Vogue* gave it seven pages in the September 2002 issue. *People, New York,* and *Bazaar* featured it as well and Miramax snapped up the movie rights.

But would any working woman with half a brain stand around trying to make store-bought pies look like home made? Of course not. We'd leave them in the supermarket container. If people don't like it, they don't have to eat the pie.

Kate is, in fact, a caricature of a working woman—a bit of a monster in fact. She neglects a friend dying of cancer, doesn't have time for her friends, shortchanges her kids, never delegates work, and never turns down an assignment. She reminds me of Joan Crawford in that old 1950s turkey, *The Best of Everything*—the career woman who can't find happiness because she's too ambitious. As Roxanne Roberts writes in the *Washington Post,* it's a familiar refrain: "No wonder it sells. It sold back in 1987, when brittle business executive Diane Keaton gave up her career and found peace (and Sam Shepard) in *Baby Boom.* It's selling 15 years later with the same subtext: work bad, mothering good."[19]

And of course, there's that great sex, which working women just don't get. A *New York Magazine* cover story, "Who's the Better Mom?" ran this subhead blazoned across a page: "Since she left the rat race, her sex life has changed. It's definitely better."[20]

The lousy sex frame was also played to the hilt in the February 2003 issue of *Atlantic Monthly.*[21] Columnist Caitlin Flanagan decreed that feminism was "a bust" because, today, working women are just too tired to have sex. She looks back with some nostalgia to the days when those 1950s wives were "getting a lot more action than many of today's most liberated and sexually experienced women." Flanagan says she asked an online sex columnist for a women's magazine if sex got better if one partner (guess who?) quits her job. The answer was an enthusiastic affirmative.

Oh really? Well, pop culture bestsellers and women's magazine columnists are not exactly the last word on the subject. When you look at more reliable scientific data, the picture is quite different. Are working women indeed too exhausted for sex? Should we all go back to the fifties where women had all the time in the world to bake cookies and dream up erotic pleasures for hubby when he got home? (That is, if they weren't too worn out from doing the laundry, the ironing, the dishes and taking care of the kids all day.)

In fact, when psychologist Abigail Stewart studied the relationship between life stress, illness, and depression in women, she found that it was the married career women with children who were best able to handle the stress.[22] Again and again, in well-designed studies, working women have been found to be healthier and less depressed than homemakers. And we know that one of the major factors in suppressing sexual desire is depression. And one longitudinal study of 500 couples (who had a child) found that although fatigue did depress sexual expression of any kind, homemakers were no less fatigued than working women.[23] The sexual satisfaction of the men was unrelated to whether their wives were at home, working part time or working more than 45 hours a week. For both men and women, the highest sexual satisfaction was among couples who both worked and experienced high rewards from their jobs. A good job, it seems, is good for your sex life.

But Flanagan claims housework is inherently women's work. "Men can be cajoled into doing all kinds of tasks, but they will not do them the way a woman would. They will bathe the children, but they will not straighten the bath mat and wring out the washcloths. They will drop a toddler off at nursery school, but they won't spend ten minutes chatting with the teacher and sorting out the art projects."

Oh? Do we really believe that all women are utterly obsessed with the domestic niceties? Are we all Martha Stewart clones? I, for one, have never in my life straightened out a bathmat. In fact, I never *bought* a bathmat. You have to scrub the damn things. Nor did I ever stop to collect the art projects. If the kids brought them home, I'd put them on the walls. They made dozens of them, so I'd just grab one out of the pile. This does not seem to have damaged their psyches.

On the subject of (prefelon days) Martha Stewart, Flanagan thinks she's a bit too stern about perfection, but gushes,

> The photography in her various publications seems to reduce all of female longing to its essential elements. A basket of flowers, a child's lawn pinafore draped across a painted rocking chair, an exceptionally white towel folded in thirds and perched in glamorous isolation on a clean and barren shelf: Most of the pictures feature a lot of sunlight, and many show rooms that are either empty of people or occupied solely by Martha, evoking the profound and enduring female desires for solitude and silence. No heterosexual man can understand this stuff, and no woman with a beating heart and an ounce of femininity can resist it.

OK, maybe I don't have an ounce of femininity, but I can never recall longing for a child's lawn pinafore draped artfully across a painted rocking chair. What world is this woman writing about? My kids draped their jeans over their beds, the floors, my bed, whatever they could find. And what is a lawn pinafore?

Flanagan believes that all women get "madder than a wet hen" if they come home to find the Legos and the pizza boxes spread over the living room. In our house, *I* am the one who leaves the mess all over the place, while my neatnik husband fumes and picks up. My daughter is the same way. She has inherited my lack of neatness genes. Doesn't seem to faze her. Her husband can change a diaper on their toddlers even quicker than she can. She finds that quite appealing.

Flanagan says she would experience a distinct lack of erotic feeling if her husband interrupted his Saturday tennis game to help out around the house. (There's a sentiment with a fifties ring to it. Does she vacuum with her pearls on while he swats backhands?) Flanagan seems to believe that men who are competent at household chores and can handle the kids are "feminized." Try to tell that to today's young dads—the ones you see everywhere these days with their babies in a snugli. They will just have a good laugh.

But the "news frame" of such stories is part of a larger, ongoing narrative. Women, if you are too smart, not docile enough (and need we say, too feminist?), bad things happen. You won't get a man, you won't have kids, you'll have lousy sex, you'll live a life of regret. Actual data show that none of this is true.

EMPTY WOMBS AND EMPTY LIVES?

If you can't panic a woman about her sex life, turn to babies. Do headlines about women's fertility—or lack of it—conceal a larger issue? Are we worried that changes in the age at which women are having children reflect larger shifts in women's lives that make us uncomfortable?

Indeed, the age at which women are giving birth for the first time has been creeping steadily upward since 1900—with a brief time out for the Baby Boom years after World War II. In 2001, Massachusetts became the first state in which more women over 30 gave birth for the first time than those under 30.[24]

Women are also getting educated at higher rates than ever before in history. Women fill more college classroom seats today than men; in little more than two decades, women have increased their share of MBAs and JDs by more than 400 percent. Since 1970, the number of women doctors has increased from 25,400 to 104,200, a 310 percent increase. There's been a 70 percent increase of women executives, administrators, and managers, compared to a 1 percent increase among men.[25]

These women obviously want to have both families and careers. And they are doing it. Nearly half the work force is female and more than half the mothers of toddlers are working.

Yet the media focus on the rash of media scare stories about women's fertility. One study that was widely misinterpreted, and one book that announced bad news, got what can only be called mega–media hype.

Young women may have been alarmed in 2002 when headlines claimed that women's fertility declines earlier than previously thought; at age 27. Because of all the publicity the study garnered, the idea still lingers that women in their late twenties have to be nervous about fertility.

But is there really a huge problem with women and fertility among 27-year-olds? Not if you look closely at the numbers.

The study, published in the journal *Human Reproduction,* does show that if you are 22, your chances of getting pregnant *in one menstrual cycle* are better than if you are 27.[26]

But is not being able to get pregnant instantly a major problem for women? Unlikely. In fact, one of the researchers told the *Montreal Gazette,* "Although we noticed a decline in female fertility in the late 20's, what we found was a decrease in the probability of becoming pregnant *per menstrual cycle* (italics mine), not in the probability of eventually achieving a pregnancy."[27]

In other words, if you're 27, there's *no* real problem with achieving a pregnancy on your second, third, or fifth try. There was even good news from the study. The probability of achieving a pregnancy was no different among women aged 27–29 than it was for women aged 30–34. But the good news was buried in most news stories and network TV reports. Instead, the stories went like this:

- Sorry, Too Late (*London Independent*).[28]
- Don't Let Fertility Slip Away (*Atlanta Journal and Constitution*).[29]
- Waiting Longer for Babies May Mean Not Having Them At All (*Sacramento Bee*).[30]

And *Time* ran a cover piece warning of "The Harsh Facts of Fertility."[31]

A similar narrative was created with the 2002 book by Sylvia Ann Hewlett titled *Creating a Life: Professional Women and the Quest for Children.*[32] It got the kind of publicity most authors only dream about. It was featured on *60 Minutes,* on *Time* and *New York* magazine covers, promoted on *Oprah,* and featured on CNN. *Time* noted: "Babies After 35: What We thought: Women can have it all—career and children—by postponing babies. Don't bet on it!"[33] The magazine then cited the Hewlett book's scare stories on declining fertility, as if it was new wisdom replacing outdated ideas. The *New York Times'* Maureen Dowd also cited the book in her 2005 article mentioned in the last chapter. She quoted Hewlett: "The rule of thumb seems to be that the more successful the woman, the less likely it is she will find a husband or bear a child."[34]

The publisher, Talk Miramax, paid the author a six-figure advance and sat back and waited for the money to roll in. It didn't. A front-page *New York Times* article declared the book to be a dud.[35] It wasn't selling.

And that was a surprise. In the past, books that bashed feminism and told women they had to be more traditional to be happy had sold well. *The Rules: Time-Tested Secrets for Capturing the Heart of Mr. Right,* a 1996 primer about how to get a man, spent 22 weeks on bestseller lists.

A number of theories were floated to explain the Hewlett book's disappointing sales. Maybe it was the critics, who complained loudly that Hewlett was overselling her theory about an "epidemic of childlessness" among high-achieving women. After all, in her own survey of 1,168 such women, two-thirds of them had children, while only a third did not. And Heather Boushey,[36] of the Center for Economic Policy Research, found high achievers to be little different than other working women. From 36 to 40, high achievers are *more* likely to be married and have kids than other female workers. (They marry later than other women.) And while Hewlett claims that high-achieving women are less likely to marry, statistics do not back up her claim. As noted earlier, high achievers are just as likely to be successfully married as other working women.[37]

But what really may have happened is that women looked around at their own lives and at those of other women and decided that Hewlett had it wrong. Her book—and the hype around it—centered on woeful tales of fortyish, high-achieving women who were miserable because they didn't have kids. Potential readers of her book probably don't see huge numbers of women whose lives are in tatters because they didn't decide to have kids in their twenties. Rather, they see lots of women planning careers, getting educated, getting married, and juggling work and family. Where are the headlines that two-thirds of high achievers do manage to have kids—even in a society that has few family-friendly policies?

As women move into their late thirties and early forties, fertility does indeed decline, on average, though many women are able to conceive. The fact that women over 40 face declining fertility is not, however, a new story. The biological clock has been an important factor in women's lives for 30 years. Hewlett thinks that many women follow a male career model and blithely cruise along assuming they will be able to have kids. They awake at about age 45 and realize, "Oops, I forgot to have kids," and are stunned when they have trouble conceiving. Perhaps some women do this—but you wonder what planet they are on. For most women, the ticking of the biological clock clangs in their ears.

Hewlett presents high-achieving women who don't have children as being unhappy. But her *Harvard Business Review* article, based on her book, presents no data—only anecdotes—on this crucial point. News stories picked up such anecdotes with little context. You can always find people whose stories back up anything you want to prove. But are *most* high-achieving women who do not have children unhappy? No. A major study of women 35 to 55, funded by the National Science Foundation and directed by Dr. Rosalind Barnett, found that childlessness did not have a significant impact on a woman's well-being.[38] (The study was the basis for our 1985 book, *Life-prints: New Patterns of Love and Work for Today's Women.*) Marriage was far more important than whether or not one had children. Childless women in this sample often went through a period of adjustment, and sometimes asked "What If?"—but by their mid-forties they were content with their choices and found their lives satisfying.

Indeed, it could be argued that women having babies later in life fits well with changing economic and demographic realities. At the turn of the century, life expectancy for women was 47.8 years and there was no contraception. In the past, women had many children so that a few could survive. Today, in the developed world, most children do survive. Modern women are going to have to support themselves for many years after their children are grown, so getting an education that will lead to a good job is an important survival tactic.

But the current scare message to young women is that they should abandon their career plans to have babies in their early twenties. If they do so, the result could be poor mental health. Research shows that good jobs have a powerful positive effect on women's emotional health; in fact, at-home women have much higher rates of depression and anxiety than do working women.[39] Women who opt out of the job market early could have a tough time getting back into high-level jobs. Research shows that one of the best predictors of poor emotional health in women is being in a dead-end job.

In fact, the worst advice we can give to young women is to relinquish serious career planning and have a baby. Most women in their late twenties to mid-thirties do not have trouble conceiving. And those in their forties and fifties who cannot conceive have other options, such as adoption. (I know many well-educated career women—married and single—who have adopted baby girls from China.) Women who opted not to have children encircle themselves with extended families and friends.

Today, there is no one-size-fits-all lifestyle, and women can find happiness and satisfaction in many ways—single or married, with and without children. Critic Katha Pollitt writes that the Hewlett book was a tome "warning women that feminism—too much confidence, too many choices, too much 'pickiness' about men—leads to lonely nights and empty bassinets."[40]

It's a familiar refrain, one to which the news media seem addicted, despite all the solid evidence to the contrary.

3
DIVORCE AND DISRUPTION

To the news media, divorce is an unmitigated disaster. Powered in part by the media, the anti-divorce movement is gathering steam. "Covenant marriages"—in which divorce is hard to get—are now legal in Louisiana and Arkansas, with bills in at least 17 other state legislatures supporting legalization. In Colorado, the legislature debated a measure that would require a year of counseling for state residents before they can get divorced, which is being vehemently opposed by groups that deal with domestic violence. President Bush suggested that funds for marriage counseling be included in the federal budget in 2003, even as he cut Head Start funds. After his 2004 reelection, he continued to support such programs.

The rationale for these measures is that divorce does irreparable harm to children. But are the children of divorce so damaged—even many years later—that we should urge unhappy couples to stay together and change our laws to make divorce harder, in the interest of children?

Based on the best available research, the answer is a resounding no. That research, however, is often ignored by the media. It's the bad news that gets all the ink. For example, massive press coverage of a very pessimistic book on divorce (including a cover piece in the *New York Times Magazine*[1] and prominent mention in an *Atlantic*[2] cover article) probably convinced untold readers that divorce was so bad that we had better do all that we can to make it hard for couples to part.

Psychologist Judith Wallerstein (with Julia Lewis and Sandra Blakeslee) argued in two best-selling books (*Second Chances* and *The Unexpected Legacy of Divorce*) that even 10 or 15 years after their parents' divorce, many young men and women still underachieve and can't handle relationships.[3] The attention the books received may lead lay readers to think it the most credible voice on the subject. The cover of the *New York Times Book Review* headlined "No Joy in Splitsville."[4] The *Times* reviewer, Margaret Talbot, scoffed at critics of the Wallerstein study, and said, "If anything, her prosperous middle-class sample should have influenced the results in a more positive direction." *The New Republic* declared unequivocally that "Wallerstein has single-handedly exploded the myth deemed to be the truth about divorce" (i.e. that children of divorce can do well emotionally).[5] The story of the mega-coverage of Wallerstein's book is a prime example of the media's inept examination of the actual research behind studies that "sound right." Too few of the stories actually examined the sample that Wallerstein used to make her conclusions. In research, your findings are only as good as the sample you select. It has to be representative of the population you are studying if it's to be valid. But the sample that Wallerstein has been following for years is small (131 people in Marin County, California). The families selected were in divorce counseling, making them atypical of the population at large. In fact, as sociologist Constance Ahrons points out, 50 percent of the men and close to half of the women were chronically depressed, sometimes suicidal, and had severe handicaps in relationships or long-standing problems controlling their rage or sexual impulses.[6] Fifteen percent were very troubled, with histories of manic depression, paranoia, and bizarre behavior. If you look at troubled people, you find trouble. Ahrons says, "That such a small sample of sixty such troubled families has made headlines and given rise to sweeping conclusions about the long-term effects of divorce only attests to our fascination with bad news . . . [R]eporting on the worst case scenarios ensures that you'll hear the worst stories." (The *Times* idea that, because these people were middle class, the findings would be credible makes it clear that the reviewer was not fully aware of the shortcomings of the sample and the severity of the subjects' problems.) Uncritical stories about the book led readers to believe that much research supports such pessimism about children of divorce. In fact, one of my Boston University colleagues told me he stayed married because of the publicity around the book. He thought he had to stay in a bad marriage for the sake of his kids. The marriage eventually broke up, and he says in retrospect that it would have been better for the children if it had ended sooner.

A DIFFERENT VIEW

The fact is that nearly all respected scholars of divorce part company with Wallerstein. In a major review of the whole body of research on divorce, psychologist Mavis Hetherington of the University of Virginia reports in *For Better or for Worse: Divorce Reconsidered* that 70 to 80 percent of children of divorce grow up to be emotionally healthy.[7] The University of Pennsylvania's Frank Furstenberg, another leading researcher, calls Wallerstein's results highly exaggerated.[8] He says that her work leads people to believe that most children who come out of a divorced family suffer permanent, lifelong damage, but the research shows that most children of divorce aren't distinguishable from the children of happily married couples.

Unfortunately, the problem with the news media is that too many stories about divorce take an "on-the-one-hand-on-the-other-hand" approach to divorce, when in fact there is indeed a consensus among serious researchers on the issue. For example, a *Philadelphia Inquirer* story in 2002, "Book Spurs Divorce Debate," cites Hetherington and her study of 1,400 families and more than 2,500 children during 30 years.[9] But then Wallerstein is quoted as another expert: "My research shows children of divorce have a very hard time growing up. They never recover from their parents' break-ups and have difficulty forming their own adult relationships." Nowhere are Wallerstein's tiny sample and flawed methodology mentioned. Readers are left thinking that two researchers of equal stature disagree. Wallerstein continues to be cited still as a leading expert on divorce.

The fact is, you can't make a categorical statement about divorce, either way. Its effects are neither always trivial nor always devastating. One 12-year study by Penn State sociologist Paul Amato found that the impact of divorce on the adult children's emotional health and intimate relationships depended *not* on the divorce per se, but rather on the combination of the level of parental conflict and divorce.[10] The adult children with the most problems were those whose parents reported high marital conflict, or those who had little conflict but divorced abruptly. It's critical to note that problems for children were *worse* in high-conflict situations when their parents did not divorce than when they did. Constance Ahrons' two-decade-long study of adult children of divorce found that, "The vast majority thrived, despite the stress and upheaval that are common in the early stages of parental divorce . . . [M]ost of the adult children felt their parents' decision to divorce had been a good one."

In a much-better designed study than Wallerstein's, University of Michigan psychologist Abigail Stewart looked at 160 families chosen from divorce case dockets, an unbiased sample.[11] She found that the end of a bad marriage proved healthy for the parents, and often also healthy for the children. Levels of tension often decreased, disorganization lessened, and kids learned to cope with difficulties. Sometimes, children formed strong, independent relationships with parents that were not overshadowed by fighting or tension.

Kids could even deal with conflict—as long as the parents were able to resist making the kids "choose sides." This divided loyalty was a major predictor of problems ahead for kids.

Implied in the media handwringing about divorce is the idea that divorce is self-perpetuating—that the children of divorce will be more likely to get involved in failed marriages themselves. Guess what? That's not true. A major study of 10,000 subjects shows little difference in the divorce rate between those whose parents divorced and those whose parents stayed married.[12]

What's the true picture? Divorce is a complicated process. Some divorces are terrible for everybody, others are liberating, depending on many issues— whether there is continuing high conflict, whether the custodial parent has enough resources, whether the family has to move, etc. But if we want to do real harm, we can club divorcing parents over the head with guilt, or rush to make unwise laws.

The Institute for American Values, a conservative think tank, advocates more covenant marriages and calls for the end of no-fault divorce. Oklahoma Governor Frank Keating and Arkansas Governor Mike Huckabee both pledged to cut divorce rates by promoting covenant marriages and through other state programs.

Will these programs help families? The reverse is probably true. State programs could keep women in marriages where there is abuse, or discourage either partner from ending a very bad marriage. The result may be to keep high conflict marriages intact—and research tells us that children in such marriages do very poorly. A major ongoing study of 20,000 children in the United States and Great Britain found that problems among children of divorce were not the result of the divorce, but arose in the period before the divorce when children were growing up in dysfunctional families.[13] (This research followed the children from before birth through the divorce proceedings.) Psychologist Robert Emery of the University of Virginia said that this study "does not mean that divorce isn't difficult, but it does mean that we have to be careful about attributing behavioral difficulties in children to the event of a divorce rather than to other aspects of family relations."[14] Small studies like Wallerstein's that look only at children after divorce have no way of knowing whether the problems that turn up are due to the divorce or to what went on before it.

The international research team conducting the major US–British study concluded that parents should not stay together "for the sake of the children" if severe problems exist in the family; it also found that intense conflict is worse for kids than divorce.

So why on earth, in the light of what we know, are we seeing a strong push for the state to get involved in deep-sixing divorce, with the media acting as cheerleaders? Many of the new initiatives are instruments of the religious right, which is trying to reintroduce an outdated view of marriage in which women must be subservient to men. It's ironic that while many conservatives give lip service to the notion of intact marriages, powerful conservative men behave in very much the same way as powerful nonconservative men. Newt Gingrich, for example, dumped wife number one while she was hospitalized for cancer and left wife number two for a younger staff aide. Robert Livingston had to withdraw from consideration for Speaker of the House after his numerous affairs were uncovered. Senator Jesse Helms was accused of trying to break up another man's marriage. Ronald Reagan, the patron saint of modern conservatism, was on his second marriage when he ran for president, as were Robert Dole and John McCain.

It would be wonderful if all marriages were happy and couples never divorced. It would also be wonderful if dollar bills fell from the sky. Federal monies for marriage counseling might be fine in times when states are flush—but to cut essential services to try to "fix" marriages is misguided. Mavis Hetherington notes that research finds that short-term programs rarely work. She says that new studies show that you have to deal with jobs, education, day care, health care—the whole constellation of a family's needs, to make a difference for troubled families.[15] We do parents and children no favors by simplistically trying to turn back the clock.

DISRUPTED BY WOMEN?

If divorce is seen as a bleak vista by the news media, what about a storyline that is far broader and bleaker. Have women's rights ruined the family and disrupted society? Is it not divorce that is problematic, but an entire universe of chaos brought on by women changing? When intellectuals—usually male—claim this is so, the media tend to accept the notion uncritically, despite the ahistorical nature of such claims and the bad science involved. Women scholars (and male ones as well) who present a more balanced picture are rarely featured in the news columns or on "talking head" opinion shows.

Take the influential social scientist James Q. Wilson. He's best known for his writings about crime and its prevention, but he jumped headlong into the culture wars. He argues (in his 2002 book *The Marriage Problem: How Our Culture Has Weakened Families*[16]) that the Enlightenment, which produced the American Revolution, constitutional democracy, and the idea that "Life, liberty and the pursuit of happiness" are among our unalienable rights, at the same time had a deleterious effect on marriage. The rights that made men free apparently made women irresponsible. In an appearance on public radio, Wilson spoke approvingly of traditional societies as better for children than marriages formed in western democracies. He specifically mentioned the Muslim world.

Traditional societies, of course, are almost by definition patriarchal and often punish women severely for sex outside of marriage, for defying strict male control over their lives, and for seeking out education and employment. But what about children? Are they really faring well in such societies? A brief look around traditional societies hardly reveals good news for children. In some parts of Africa, an AIDS epidemic has killed millions of children and orphaned millions more, because women do not have the right to demand that their husbands use condoms when they have frequented prostitutes. In parts of Asia, female children are sold into sexual slavery by their parents. Children's advocates say that, in the third world, so many children die every day that it's the equivalent of four jumbo jets crashing daily.

In fact, the history of childhood in the premodern world and in traditional societies, far from being a story of safe havens for children, has been a grim catalogue of horrors. But the news media tend to overlook this fact, because of their ahistoric nature. It's the Nostalgia Trap at work again.

While exaggerating the blessings of traditional societies, James Q. Wilson also overstates the woes of modern childhood. Like others in the so-called "marriage movement," he takes an extremely pessimistic view of any relationships other than traditional marriage. (This pessimism also fuels the drive for a constitutional amendment outlawing same-sex marriage.)

Wilson presents an unremittingly bleak picture of the prospects of children raised in single-parent families. But we need to look at the picture through a complex lens. Almost all social science data show that SES—socioeconomic status—is the strongest predictor of almost any index of child welfare. The combination of poverty and having only a single parent—usually a woman—can be devastating for kids. But is promoting marriage an answer? Do we really want the 16-year-old pregnant girl in the inner city to marry her drug-dealer boyfriend? Wouldn't we be better off trying to insure that 16-year-olds don't get pregnant?

Wilson also ignores the dark side of marriage. Though overall, both adults and children get a host of benefits from good marriages, the situation for those in bad marriages is quite the opposite. There is overwhelming evidence, points out family historian Stephanie Coontz, that high conflict in marriage, or even silent withdrawal coupled with contempt, damages children more than divorce or growing up in a single-parent family.[17] For example, teens in two-parent families who have a poor relationship with their fathers are more likely to abuse drugs that those in single-parent families.

Simple-minded policies to make people stay married just won't work. As essayist Michael Ignatieff notes, "There is a real tyranny in the 'family values' espoused by so much of North American popular entertainment, pulpit sentiment, and political homily."[18] I'd add the news media to the list. It makes everyone who doesn't fit a Disneyized version of the perfect nuclear family feel "inadequate, ashamed or downright guilty."

4
SUFFER THE LITTLE CHILDREN

Perhaps the most damaging myth that the media endlessly promote is the idea that nonmaternal care—day care—is harmful to children. If mothers are not with their children every waking hour, the warning goes, children will suffer greatly. It's a narrative that surfaces again and again in many different guises.

This idea was the leit-motif in one of the major news stories about families in recent years—the "nanny murder case." In that instance, a Massachusetts doctor, Deborah Eappen, had left her infant son in the care of a young British nanny, Louise Woodward, who was convicted in 1997 of shaking the baby to death. The storm of vituperation that rolled over the mother in the media—and especially on talk radio—was overwhelming. She was accused coast to coast of being a bad mother. Handing her child over to a nanny was tantamount to child abuse.

The Nanny Trial became a Grimm's Fairy Tale—except this time it was aimed at parents, not children. As the *St. Louis Post Dispatch* noted in a 1997 editorial, "For some, Woodward wasn't the only one responsible for Matthew's death."[1] The real criminal was Deborah Eappen, the mother who had left her child in the care of another. She committed the sin of "wanting it all," of thinking that she could have a family and a job at the same time. It was her arrogance that led her to practice her profession when the family didn't need the money. She left her child in the hands of a stranger. She might as well have killed little Matthew herself. From Medea to Susan Smith, something about women killing children shakes the social order. Such crimes are almost inevitably viewed as glimpses into the Zeitgeist. That so many see the nanny case as proof that women who work outside the home put their children's lives at risk is sobering evidence of a feminist backlash.

Most fairy tales are homey fables with instructive scare stories tucked inside. Grandma is really a wolf, beautiful stepmothers turn into witches with poisoned apples, and trolls live under perfectly innocent bridges. The message many people took from the trial of Louise Woodward is that danger lurks everywhere. Even a charming British nanny spells danger. *Mary Poppins Kills Your Baby* isn't in anybody's Little Golden Books collection.

Several mothers interviewed on television said that they felt they could never leave their babies again. Others began to scrutinize their au pairs with new eyes. *New York Times* pundit William Safire weighed in with the opinion that it's better to leave your kids with "strange" relatives than with relative strangers.[2]

While the Matthew Eappen story became an international media firestorm, another terrible story from the same state got absolutely no attention from the national media. A ten-year-old boy in Massachusetts playing outside while in the care of his grandmother was kidnapped, then raped and murdered by pedophiles. There were no stories accusing the grandmother of being a terrible person—as indeed, there should not have been. There were no editorials saying, *Why wasn't this boy in an afterschool program? Then this tragedy never would have happened.*

The fact is, research shows that, overwhelmingly, most injuries to children occur when they are home, supervised by their parents, not when they are in day care or with nannies. Having your au pair kill your child is a very rare event, comparable to a lightning strike. I employed a lot of babysitters, but the various injuries my kids suffered were all on my watch. The fly ball on the head, the sliced foot on the beach, the fall off the bike, the tons of stitches—who was in charge? Not the sitters. Me.

Throughout history, few infants have been cared for solely by their parents. Kinfolk, neighbors, hired hands, live-in help, and slaves all cared for children, and often the children flourished. Millions of nannies and au pairs and day care workers have given loyal, loving care to children. One reason the nanny murder drew so much attention was because it was so rare.

Perhaps one reason so many people wanted to see Louise Woodward declared innocent is because we don't want to believe that menace could come in so proper a package. If, indeed, we could believe that there was a prior injury, and the parents had just been derelict in spotting it, we could breathe easier. Because, in our heart of hearts, we know *we* wouldn't make that mistake. I remember when my kids were very young, each time I read of some tragedy that befell a child, I'd eagerly scan the story for traces of a parental misstep. Aha! They let him play near a pond. They didn't make sure the screens were tight. They waited too long to take his temp. I wouldn't do that! This parental anxiety probably encourages readers to buy into "bad mommy" stories.

So thinking a particular set of parents was at fault in the nanny case is reassuring. But if the guilty party was a young woman like Louise Woodward—

the person all us middle-class parents would hire in a minute—then we're all vulnerable.

What was the legacy of the massive coverage of the nanny trial? Did it lead to a national discussion of the sparse resources we allocate to child care? No. The only result was another layer of anxiety laid on working parents' heads, especially working mothers.

The Nostalgia Trap is at work here, and journalists fall right into it. The late Michael Kelly, former editor of the *Atlantic,* wrote in a *Boston Globe* op ed that we are engaged in a "radical experiment on our children" because children are not always at home with a parent.[3] Once again, the 1950s serves as the normative human experience.

But is it? Not at all. The fifties' ideal of one woman alone in a single-family house raising her children is far from the historical norm. Children have always had multiple caretakers, and not just family members. Children raised communally in Israeli kibbituzes are models of health. Female slaves raised white children in the Old South; immigrant girls worked as nannies in Victorian homes in the North. In upper-class England, children are sent to boarding schools at early ages; in colonial New England, boarders were taken in to help with farm chores and child care, and it was a common practice in Puritan colonies for families to send their children to other families to be raised so that they would be "godfearing." For most of history, in hunter-gatherer societies, children were cared for by groups of adults. Before the modern era, half of all children could expect to suffer the death of one or both parents and were raised by distant relatives or strangers. (Read *Jane Eyre,* read *Dickens.*) The nuclear family is a modern invention, not a historical fact.[4] Day care is simply one of many permutations in a checkered pantheon of ways of caring for children, not some radical break with the past.

There are simply no data to support claims that it is "better" for children for one parent to be at home full time. University of Michigan psychologist Lois Hoffman examined fifty years of studies of the children of working mothers—no subject was studied more—and found no significant difference on any measure of child development between the children of working mothers and mothers at home.[5]

Still, it is the media's usual assumption that motherhood is simply "natural" for women, that all women should be blissfully happy at home, and those who go out to work are "bad mommies." This can make for very skewed personal decisions. Take the case of Andrea Yates, the Texas woman who drowned her five children. Why was Andrea Yates at home caring for five young children when it was known that she had a history of suicidal depression and had been on anti-psychotic drugs? Was it because of her husband's belief—and society's—that a mother's place is in the home, no matter what? If we could accept the fact that outside child care is as necessary for mothers and children as "mothercare," maybe we wouldn't put so much stress on mothers. If Andrea Yates wasn't so hard-pressed and isolated, if she wasn't trying to care for and home school her kids and cope with crippling postpartum psychosis, this tragedy might not have happened.

We've known for a long time that being at home with young kids can take a toll on women. That fact was documented in the 1970s when psychologist Marcia Guttentag was studying the causes of the very high level of psychiatric symptoms among homemakers.[6] She concluded, "There's nothing more depressing than a houseful of young children."

But where were the editorials calling for more funding for day care in the wake of the Yates tragedy? I didn't see them.

In fact, good news about day care is practically nonexistent in the news media, while bad news is everywhere. A good example is the coverage of one of the largest, best-designed studies of children ever done in the United States.

A FRAGILE BOND?

Because of concerns about whether day care interfered with a child's bond, or attachment, with its mother, the federal National Institute of Child Health and Human Development (NICHD) is currently conducting a large, expensive, and very well designed study of children from infancy onward.[7] It is following some 1,110 children at ten sites around the country from birth to adulthood.

The initial reports were very encouraging. At five and fourteen months, the researchers found, infants in day care were securely attached to their mothers. There was virtually no difference in attachment whether children were at home, cared for by a mother or father, or in day care or cared for by a relative.

You'd have thought that this would be huge news, after all the scare stories: a major national study showing that even infants in day care were securely attached to their mothers. It should have been headlined in every paper across the nation. It wasn't.

A week after the findings were announced, I did a Lexis search and found only a dozen references to the NICHD study (including a very good, very detailed *New York Times* piece). But six of those—fully half—were written by myself and Dr. Rosalind Barnett. The silence of the media on the good news about day care was stunning. I compared that to references in Lexis to the book *Children First,* by British psychologist Penelope Leach, which claimed that women should not work until their children were eight years old because of concern over attachment disorder.[8] I found nearly three hundred references to Leach in the media. (Leach had also been the subject of a cover profile in the *New York Times Magazine.*[9])

I would guess that, today, most readers of the American media do not know that a major study has found that even infants in day care are securely attached to their mothers. Who could fault them? The media can hardly find a "news frame" on the issue that isn't really a "bad news" frame.

Will this ever change? Read on.

BULLY BOYS AND GIRLS

The major NICHD study mentioned above is ongoing, so we can expect bulletins from time to time at different periods of the children's lives.[10] One of those bulletins (in the spring of 2001, when the kids were preschoolers) unearthed some good news and some not-so-good news about kids in day care. But, as usual, the bad news got all the media attention.

At this juncture, the researchers had found that children in high-quality care scored higher on tests of language, memory, and other skills than did children of stay-at-home mothers or children in lower-quality day care. Professor Robert C. Pianta of the University of Virginia, an investigator on the project, told the *Los Angeles Times,* "There are quite convincing findings that the quality of child care has a positive association with a range of social and academic skills."[11]

But did this news get all the headlines? No indeed. It was the *other* finding that got the ink. Seventeen percent of children in day care more than 30 hours per week were said to be more aggressive and disobedient than children who were in day care for fewer hours.

The media had a field day, with headlines implying that kids in day care are at great risk for becoming aggressive, mean bullies—monsters, in fact. Typical of many "bullies" headlines were these: "Connecting the Dots Between Day Care and Bullies" (*Denver Post*)[12]; "Day Care Turns Out Bullies" (*Ottawa Citizen*).[13]

And a nationally syndicated cartoon showed a couple of kids walking through a school corridor looking warily at another kid behind them. One boy says to his friend, "Watch out for the new kid. I heard he did hard time at the weenie tots day care center." (See fig. 1.)

It's not surprising that some parents felt more than a touch of panic at this news. What were they doing to their children by sending them to day care?

FIG. I

Were the kids going to turn into monsters—Jeffrey Dahmers or the Columbine Killers? Were their children going to turn out to be rotten people, despite all their good efforts?

Once again, the media was hyping sensational bad news. Great headlines. Terrific coverlines. But parents worried about their kids needed to take a deep breath—and look both at the real facts of this study *and* at the nature of scientific research and statistics.

The study reported that only 6 percent of children who spent fewer hours in child care were regarded as more aggressive to other children, as compared to 17 percent in longer-hour day care. This all sounds quite alarming. But what do these findings really mean?

First of all, this was a large study, looking at many factors about the experience of kids in day care, so, does the aggression finding really mean anything? Researchers needed to look much deeper to find out. Exactly what was the behavior that caregivers and teachers observed? In fact, here's the behavior that could get you labeled aggressive, if you were a kid: argues, brags, talks too much, shows off, teases, stubborn, fights, threatens, attacks, loud, temper.

What preschooler on the planet hasn't displayed some of the above? Teasing? Bragging? Being stubborn? In fact, if a little kid isn't stubborn at times, he or she violates the laws of nature.

And what about talking back and disobeying? Maybe it was the nature of these kids that was operating here. After all, the day-care kids had higher cognitive and verbal skills than the average at-home kid. It could be that smart, verbal kids talk back more and are harder to control than other kids. There's a big difference between being a bully and being a kid who knows how to test the limits of teachers—or who is able to use verbal skills to get what he or she wants from other children. Maybe at-home kids are more passive because they don't have to deal with a bunch of other kids a lot of the time, and don't have to develop verbal skills to get what they want.

What the study does *not* say is that most children in long-hour day care are aggressive. While 17 percent is a large enough number to deserve more study, the great majority of children in day care for over 30 hours are *not* aggressive, demanding, or bullying.

And the children who *are* more aggressive, are they out-of-control terrors, perhaps destined to shoot up their classrooms in later years? No. The aggression was in the "normal" range, the researchers said, not requiring professional attention. Too little, in fact, was known about the finding to say much about it. As Berkeley psychologist Philip Cowan noted:

> We don't know whether this is the kind of assertive aggression that young kids, especially boys, normatively display at ages 3–5 or whether we're talking about beating other kids up. We don't know whether the highly aggressive kids at age five will be highly aggressive later. Perhaps the low aggressive youngsters in these studies haven't had enough experience in large groups to know how to take care of themselves appropriately. That is, it may be that the low aggression kids have a problem. There's lots we don't know.[14]

Cowan cautions, "We need to be more careful what we say to parents and policy makers on the basis of these data."

In fact, when you add context and understanding to what the researchers found, there was no reason for alarm. The news media, however, exercised hardly any caution, opting instead for the sensational "bully" headlines.

WHOSE AGENDA?

Perhaps most important, was there an ideological side to the whole issue? The loudest voice about the aggression finding was made by the controversial researcher Jay Belsky, now at a London University. In 1986, he wrote an article that created a furor.[15] He suggested that day care for very young children could harm the "attachment" (or bond) between mother and child. The media ran wild with that idea, and professionals worried. As I've said, concern about the trauma that daily separation from their working mothers might have on children was one of the reasons that the NICHD study was launched in the first place. The study found, of course, that infants in day care were securely attached to their mothers.

We probably should have guessed that result in advance. In the 1930s, Dr. John Bowlby did the research on which the whole idea of "maternal deprivation" was based.[16] It came from studies of orphans who lay for hours on end in their cribs with no human contact. Not surprisingly, they wound up with serious developmental problems. But at the same time, Bowlby studied the children of women who worked in factories, and these children were perfectly normal.

The whole "attachment" issue turned out to be very much overblown. So we have to ask, was Belsky riding the same old hobbyhorse again, and getting a lot of press for doing so? Some of his fellow researchers thought so. Belsky held a press conference to report the data over the objections of most of his colleagues in the study, before the data had been discussed and reviewed by his peers. Few articles I found reported this controversy.

There's another important issue involved. Does day care "cause" whatever aggression was found, or is the agression the result of other factors? If some kids do have real behavior problems, they could be due not to day care per se, but to the fact that underpaid day care workers aren't trained to deal with children's emotional issues. Maybe the kids' parents are just stressed out and are communicating this to their kids. Researchers suggest that this parental stress could be the causative factor in kids' acting out.

This would hardly be surprising. Unlike European societies, the United States has made little societal accommodation for the fact that nearly 70 percent of parents today are working. There is little government-subsidized day care, as there is in France and Sweden. Maternity and paternity leaves are short and usually unpaid, and vacation time is shrinking for American workers.

The "stressed-parent" hypothesis is made more likely by the fact that there is no inevitable link between nonmaternal child care and aggression. Studies of children raised in Israeli kibbutzes found these children quite the opposite of aggressive.[17] They were more cooperative and peer-oriented than other children. And these kids spent more hours away from their mothers than most kids anywhere—often sleeping at night in "children's houses."

But Belsky said, in his press conference, that parents ought to work less. Another researcher chided him, saying that he shouldn't be making policy statements at this stage when so much more work needed to be done. If parental stress can cause kids to be aggressive, working less could exacerbate such stress. That would be especially true if cutting down hours at work meant financial problems for parents. It could cause a vicious spiral. The parents work less, run into financial problems, stress out more, and their kids wind up worse off.

All these complexities mean we have to know a lot more before coming up with concrete suggestions for how long parents should—or should not—work.

What we should do is focus our energies on giving day care providers more training in the emotional needs of children. In the Scandinavian countries, day care workers often have several years of training and are well paid. In the United States, day care is one of the lowest-paid professions, meaning that too many day care workers are unskilled and ill equipped to deal with kids' needs.

Raising children is a complex process, and there's no style of parenting that is problem-free. When middle-class mothers stayed home in the 1950s, social critics coined the term "momism" and said that American children were selfish and spoiled because of their overprotective mothers.[18] Some went so far as to say that indulgent mothers were the reason that American servicemen broke under torture in Korea.

Today, it's working women who are said to be harming their children, by not spending their every waking moment "relating" to their kids. The fact is, kids generally do just fine when their mothers are at home, and just fine when their mothers are working, if the mothers are happy with their choices. So, if you're a working parent, don't panic over day care. Stay tuned to discover what researchers come up with when they examine these issues more thoroughly. But keep in mind, the media are nothing if not inventive about finding new scare stories to drive working women to distraction.

FALLING INTO THE TRAP

The media handle nothing so badly as research about women and children. Sometimes it's from ignorance, but sometimes it's from the need to make a story more "sexy" than it really is. Scientific studies are often boringly balanced and laced with caveats—"Howevers" and "on-the-other-hands." The incredible competitive pressures facing most publications too often tempt editors and writers to make far too much of a story that needs those caveats to give an accurate reflection of reality. They easily get lost in the pursuit of a good headline, a jazzy lead. The world of research is dotted with "tiger traps" for those looking for a good story—concealed holes in the ground with jagged edges into which one can easily stumble. Writers often do. Here are the some of mistakes they make:

- *False links.* Making connections when there aren't any and inferring causation from correlation. A study may indeed find that people with red hair eat more apples than people with black hair. That does not mean, however, that having red hair is the cause of a taste for apples.
- *Generalizing from anecdotes.* This is a rampant abuse. Most likely you have read one of those stores that begins, "Martha chewed on her pencil, her head throbbing. She was trying to finish her final report, but she couldn't help thinking about two-year-old Jason, at the day care center." The reader goes on to read about how Martha and a few of her friends are miserable because they are not spending 24 hours a day with their children. But is Martha typical of most mothers? You will never know, because the writer (or her editor) made her mind up after hearing a few stories, and then fit the article around those anecdotes. Or maybe the storyline was decided on in advance, and the writer sought stories to fit the desired narrative. Ask yourself. Have you *ever* read a story that began, "Martha concentrated on her report, secure in the knowledge that her child was doing well in day care, and knowing as well that she spent lots of time with her child." (I was that sort of Martha. My husband and I, for example, both worked, but we decided that we would not take jobs that involved a lot of travel, and that we would center our social life on the family. We knew our kids were being well cared for by responsible people when we weren't there.)
- *Picking out one statistic to highlight that fits the story.* You find this all the time in magazine stories. The headline, the lead, the graphics— in fact the entire thrust of the story—are based on new and usually startling statistics. No critics are quoted—or if they are, they are given a line or two far down in the story.
- *Small, unrepresentative samples.* Building major stories on studies that are too small or too badly designed to be valid.
- *Backpedaling.* Making sweeping claims early in the story that are then backed away from.
- *Misleading headlines and graphics.* Not matching headlines and graphics to the actual facts or importance of the story.

- *Factoid sinkholes.* Questionable "facts" migrating to the background paragraphs of stories as uncontested fact.
- *Good news is no news.* Ignoring positive stories.

One stunning example of scary graphics and backpedaling is a *New York Times Magazine* cover story on the problems facing parents who adopt Romanian orphans.[19] The magazine cover features a stark, somewhat out-of-focus photograph of a young boy, his mouth opened in a scream of anguish. The photograph is all stark blacks, whites, and grays, as if to underline the message of the headline, that stands out in stark white letters: *"Disturbed, detached, unreachable."*

This child is clearly in trouble. Beneath the headline is an explanatory coverline—clearly concocted to send a cold chill down the spine of every working mother who reads it: *"Children adopted by Americans from the worst European orphanages may be telling us not only about the extreme trauma of parental deprivation but also about the more routine separation of parent and child."*

This, mind you, is a story about Romanian orphans. It is a legitimate story, because Americans who have adopted these children, it turns out, are having many problems with the children's socialization. Some have severe behavior problems, hit or bite their siblings or adoptive parents, some can't relate to other children or adults, some seem so locked away in a world inside their heads that they are, as the headline claims, *unreachable.*

A very interesting story, I'd read it.

But maybe not enough people would.

How to solve that problem, if you are an editor or writer? Simple. Link the orphans up with working mothers. Raise the specter of harm to children of everyday Americans and their own children. Now that *really* ups the ante. Suggest that the severe emotional problems of these traumatized children are somehow connected to "the routine separations of parent and child."

What does that mean? You don't have to be Einstein to figure it out. Now you've got a real sexy story. Scare working mothers out of their shorts. They will pay attention.

But, in fact, do the problems of children adopted from the most miserable orphanages of Eastern Europe have *any* connection with the lives of children of working mothers? As it turns out, not at all. And the story itself even says so. But not before scaring the bejesus out of a lot of us. The story, in fact, sets us up for quite the opposite conclusion.

The "nut graf" of the story—the one that explains to the reader what it is all about—reads thusly: *"Mother-child separations are part of the warp and woof of life these days, and so are our worries about them. The research on Eastern European adoptees matters not only to them and their parents but also to many of the rest of us as well."*

And why? *"The traumatized orphans adopted from Eastern Europe have not only brought despair to some American couples but have also become Exhibit A for those who argue that a mother's place is with her child."*

As the article progresses, we hear chilling tales of "attachment disorder" suffered by these orphans. They were horribly neglected in the state-run orphanages, often deprived of any human touch, cuddling, hugging—all the things that create in children a sense that they are loved, that they are connected to other people, and that they can love in return.

At this point, readers are undoubtedly trembling: *Oh God, I leave Little Sara at day care five days a week. Is she going to turn out like this?*

And then, suddenly, after all the *sturm* and *drang,* the backpedal appears. Just as we are prepared to believe that, yes, there is a link between these orphans and the children of working mothers, the story abruptly changes direction. After the flashy, foreboding graphics, the coverline hinting darkly at harm, the theme paragraph graph hinting at connections between orphans and ordinary kids, the author starts to backpedal like mad, citing the major federal study of day care I wrote about in the last chapter: "While there are some negative effects of child care, they are quite small—statistical flutters . . . [T]here were *not* significant differences in attachment related to child care participation." (Italics added)

Statistical flutters? A "flutter" was the entire basis for the graphics, the headline, the theme paragraph, the scary stuff? All of these pyrotechnics leading up to—a statistical flutter?

But never mind. The magazine is not apologizing. "However small such effects might be, it may not do to ignore them."

Why the hell not? If there's no connection that could or would be made by anyone with even an iota of scientific sophistication, if the whole story is based on a false pretense, why not ignore it? The translation of that last line is *There's no trend and no story, but we're doing it anyhow.*

HAS WORK BECOME HOME?

Another "bad news about women and children" tale reflects the same sloppy handling of research data by journalists. The book *The Time Bind* by Arlie Hochschild[20] got massive media coverage, including a *Newsweek* cover story[21] and many newspaper stories.

The book has a startling thesis: Women are so much happier at work than at home—where they face major stress—that they are spending more time at work than at home. A historic reversal has occurred, the author claimed. Where once home had been a refuge from work, where people enjoyed their families, their friends, and unwound from the stresses of work, all that has reversed. Work has become home, and home has become work. Women like being at work so much that they are spending more time there, and as a result, children are being neglected, Hochschild implies. The opening of the *Newsweek* article echoes this idea: "Parents who race in the door at 7:30 p.m. and head straight for the fax machine are making it perfectly clear where their loyalties lie and the kids are showing the scars."

This certainly would scare readers about the future of working women and their children. But, in fact, was Hochschild right? Are women spending more time at home than at work? The numbers have to be right, or the whole thesis falls apart. A closer look by Dr. Rosalind Barnett of Brandeis revealed a much less "sexy" story than the one the media was telling. How solid were Hochschild's data? Not very.

Hochschild studied only one company, called "Americo," and she based all her findings on the people she interviewed at this company. How many people did she interview? 130. And how many people reflected the trend on which her entire book—and a slew of news stories and magazine articles—were based? Hochschild writes, "Overall, this 'reversal' was a predominant pattern in about a fifth of Americo families, and an important theme in over half of them."

This is a major trend? For 20 percent of the 130 people she interviewed—26 people—this pattern was "predominant." *Eighty percent* of the sample did not exhibit this pattern as the major one in their lives. If the media had looked more carefully at these figures, there might have been fewer headlines and cover stories trumpeting a major new trend. But such caveats often get lost. The misreporting by the media lives forever in the age of the internet, and every reporter doing a story about work and family issues probably comes across the story of *The Time Bind* when he or she begins researching. I was reading Todd Gitlin's excellent book *Media Unlimited: How the Torrent of Images and Sounds Overwhelms Our Lives,* and found this line: "Some working women, beset by conflict at home, actually prefer working longer hours."[22] He cities *The Time Bind* as the source of this "fact." A perfect example of how the news media make flawed research immortal.

5

THE MOMMY DIARIES

Call them "The Mommy Diaries"—the news frames and narratives that reflect our cultural ambivalence about just what—and who—mothers should be.

The first thing you notice in stories about mothers is that women cease to exist as stand-alone, fully developed human individuals. They are mommies, and the focus is always on their children: Are they happy? Neglected? Loved? Are their verbal skills adequate? Are they firmly attached? Are they underperforming in school? Will they get into Harvard?

Mothers are judged on how well their children do in a wide range of areas—their weight, their emotional adjustment, how many hours of TV they watch, their school achievement, how many friends they have, etc., etc. In fact, what has been called the "New Traditionalism" or the "New Momism" reduces mothers to the sum of their children's parts. As Susan J. Douglas and Meredith W. Michaels point out in *The Mommy Myth,* these ideas "redefine all women, first and foremost, through their relationships to children. Thus, being a citizen, a worker a governor, an actress, a first lady, all are supposed to take a backseat to motherhood. (Remember how people questioned whether Hillary Clinton was truly maternal because she had only one child?)"[1] The new models of perfect motherhood insist that women have to be always adoring, flawless mothers before they do anything else. As critic Letty Cotton Pogrebin puts it, "You can go be a CEO and a good one, but if you're not making a themed birthday party you're not a good mother, and thus, you are a failure."[2] Rarely do men vanish as individuals in the news media in the way that women who become mothers do.

There are several narratives about mothers popular in the news media today. They include:

• Mothers are dangerous and not to be trusted. Their actions imperil their children.
• Mothers are selfish, more interested in themselves than their children.

- The Mommy Wars are raging, with at-home and working mothers at each other's throats.
- Women Can't Have It All—a corollary to the news frame that I examined in an earlier chapter, that Women Are Always Going Home.

Interestingly, one mommy narrative that has vanished from the mainstream media since I wrote my last media critique in 1996 is The Welfare Queen, the greedy, drug-addicted, child-neglecting, Cadillac-driving nightmare of the middle class. For the most part, welfare mothers have simply vanished from the great radar screen of the news media. Where are they? Jason De Parle, the *New York Times* writer who has made welfare his beat, gives the answer in his book, *American Dream, Three Women, Ten Kids, and a Nation's Drive to End Welfare,* which follows three mothers through the end of federal child welfare payments.[3] They are in menial jobs that don't pay enough for them to live on, are having trouble finding child care and seeing the dream of the title slip further and further away from their grasp.

Dangerous Mothers are a current obsession with the news media. Once upon a time, neglectful or even crazy mothers were basically a local story—and then only if the offense was horrific, like murder. Today, with 24-hour cable news and the internet, bad mothers seem to be everywhere. When Susan Smith let her three children drown in the back of a car in South Carolina after she watched it roll into a lake, when a mentally ill woman dropped her three children into San Francisco Bay, when Andrea Yates drowned her five children in a bathtub in Texas in the grip of postpartum psychosis, when Hedda Nussbaum failed to protect her six-year-old daughter from being brutally murdered in New York by her adoptive father, these became instant national stories. The massive, constant coverage of these stories, and many others like them, I believe, have changed the way we think about mothers. While we still like to idealize mommies, suspicion has crept in. We have become less tolerant of mothers' rights.

As the moral authority of mothers erodes, thanks in part to the mass media, we are seeing more and more attempts to police mothering. Prosecutors bring charges against women who are addicted to drugs or alcohol because they may be endangering their babies. (Such well-publicized cases, of course, may very well scare addicted women away from seeking help.) One wonders how far this will go. Could a pregnant woman seen sipping white wine in a restaurant be fingered by a fellow diner who calls 911? Since obesity could adversely affect a fetus, could a judge order a woman to have her jaw wired during pregnancy and fed through a tube? Can a mother who smokes be indicted? (When my daughter was pregnant, she read a book that said if she craved a sweet, she could just chew it and spit it out. "Are you going to do that?" I asked, incredulously. "I'm pregnant, I'm not stupid," she replied.)

If this scenario sounds fanciful, consider that, since 1985, more than 200 US women have been prosecuted on charges that their drug use endangered their fetus.[4] Interestingly, most arrests were of black and Latina women. As Douglas and Michaels point out, "No comparable arrests were made, at country clubs, say, of mothers who took Valium, smoked or drank excessively."[5]

Today, some argue that taking a birth control pill could harm a nonpregnant woman's future children (although there are no data to show this is so.) More alarming, some states are considering legislation that would outlaw most forms of birth control. If you read the fine print of such bills, they ban any substance that could affect the live birth of not just an existing fetus, but one that might *someday* exist. (See chapter 11 for details.) Could a prosecutor bring charges against a woman using a birth control pill on the grounds that she was endangering a future fetus? That sounds outrageous, but that's indeed what some proposed legislation would allow.

The news frame of the Dangerous Mommy is alive and well, and unfortunately does not correct itself by updated reporting. A few years back, the media hyped the specter of millions of terribly addicted "crack babies" that would result from drug addiction among poor women. It didn't happen. In fact, well-designed research showed no consistent relationship between a mother's cocaine use and long-term deficiencies in her child. Nonetheless, Douglas and Michaels note, "These subsequent studies correcting the myth of the crack baby got zero coverage." And, they say, this story frame contributed significantly to "a vigilante culture in which mothers have to be carefully policed, because they are, potentially, their children's worst enemies. While this was hardly the intent of the news media, the parade of maternal delinquents reinforced an increasingly narrow form of acceptable behavior that helped . . . to standardize the rules of the New Momism."[6]

SELFISH, SELFISH, SELFISH!

Selfish parents and the decline of the family are two phrases that have moved into the "background" paragraphs of news stories. They are considered to be "facts" so obvious that they need not be called the "alleged" decline or the "alleged" selfishness, journalistic shorthand that signals to the reader that this is what someone claims but it is not necessarily fact.

When I tried to plug the words "selfish" and "parents" in the Nexis database over a two-year period, I was told I could not access the material, because I would get more than a thousand documents. Selfish parents are everywhere in the media, to wit: "Selfish parents need to grow up" (*The Atlanta Journal and Constitution*)[7]; "Selfish parents just won't sacrifice for kids" (*Chicago Sun Times*).[8]

As for family decline, it's omnipresent in the media. I plugged the words "family breakdown" into the Nexis data base for the previous two years, and once again wasn't able to get specific citations because there were more than a thousand references.

But are parents more selfish today they there were in 1776? or 1895? or 1955? When *wasn't* the family declining? In 1928 the best-known child psychologist of the day predicted that marriage would be finished by 1977. And in 1954, a *Newsweek* cover story trumpeted "Our Teenagers are out of control."[9] Sound familiar? You can read the same sentiments from social critics in 1850 and 1950. Families—and society—are going to hell in a handcart.

Enter the modern media, whose historical memory is about half a nanosecond. Historian Stephanie Coontz, author of *The Way We Never Were: American Families and the Nostalgia Trap*—a veritable fountain of information about the real American family—notes that we are constantly bombarded with little snippets of information known as factoids. "The word suggests little fragments of data, broken off from their original planetary moorings, zinging merrily through space and occasionally hurtling down into our atmosphere in a fleeting arc of light."[10] (Describes the sound bite to a T, doesn't it?)

She also points out that news outlets need to market their wares as "new." Old doesn't sell. So the decline of the family has to be packaged as a trend, a novel phenomenon.

But a measured analysis that takes a long look back through history isn't the stuff of headlines. The 24-hour-media is more and more fueled by factoids and sound bites and by the need for people to scream at each other on cable talk shows about the latest information chunklet that soars into view. Readers and viewers sometimes get the idea that nothing exists but the present, which is always in chaos.

The current chaos always stands out in sharp relief against the presumed sunniness of the past. How many readers are aware that in the late nineteenth century, 20 percent of American children were in orphanages? In colonial times, there was no such thing as a "divorce rate." But were families stable? Hardly. High death rates meant that the average length of marriage was 12 years. One third to half of all children lost at least one parent before 21.[11]

And our ancestors certainly understood illegitimacy very well. It wasn't invented by modern ghetto teenagers. In postrevolutionary Concord, Mass., one-third of the babies were born out of wedlock.[12] And the diary of a sixteenth-century New England midwife noted that 38 percent of the 814 birthings she attended were the result of extramarital conception. (Her story was chronicled by historian Laurel Thatcher Ulrich in *A Midwife's Tale*.)[13] The law required that midwives obtain from an unmarried woman in labor the name of the father of the child, since the court required his identity so that the town would not have to support the "bastard." One young man described in the midwife's diary was an illegitimate child, acknowledged and financially supported by a prominent judge, who was a married man. And the midwife heard from the lips of one pregnant woman whose child she was delivering that it had been fathered out of wedlock by *her own son*. Illegitimacy and sex outside of marriage, it seems, are as American as apple pie.

In fact, recent US census data show that American families are becoming more "traditional." No, not like Ozzie and Harriet. The new data tell us that American families are becoming more as they were a century ago—or two centuries ago—rather than like the recent past. The Census Bureau announced in 2001 that nuclear families had dropped below 25 percent of all households, and the trend continues. Multiple family forms are now the rule in American society, not the exception.[14]

Our colonial forebears would have understood blended modern families better than they would have understood Ozzie and Harriet. Our families are blended by divorce; theirs were blended by death. Serial marriages were common for men, who often lost wives in childbirth. And a way of life that was largely agricultural meant that households were often made up of many people—not just kin but others who came to help work the land or maintain the household. Blended families were the norm.

And how did children fare? In many cases, worse than the children of today's divorces, because parents are still available to these kids. When parents died, children were at the mercy of kin, or strangers. In New England towns in the eighteenth century, mentally ill parents were auctioned off to local farmers or tradesman who would use the labor of the children for free. In 1820, half the laborers in factories were children under 11. On farms, children began to work as soon as they could walk. Mothers often worked sunup to sundown on farm chores—they were not available to supervise children, who were usually in the care of siblings. Thousands of children drowned in streams, were killed by horses and other farm animals, or suffered other accidents.[15] The daily lives of children often involved a great deal of risk. My son's wife's mother, for example, rode to school with her two siblings in rural Nebraska, all on one horse. No parent was around to supervise.

In fact, although today's parents have nightmares about their children being kidnapped by strangers, or stalked by internet predators, in actual fact such events are very, very rare. Children are probably safer today than in the past.

As the media repeatedly chant about the decline of the family, scientific research continues to paint the opposite picture. A study published in the journal *Demography* in 2001, reports that despite a sharp increase in the number of dual-career families, today's children spend significantly more time with their parents than children did two decades ago.[16]

The study, by scientists at the University of Michigan's Institute for Social Research, showed that, in 1981, children between the ages of 3 and 12 in two-parent families spent about 25 hours a week with their mothers. In 1997 they spent 31 hours. The time spent by fathers increased from 19 to 23 hours a week.

Sociologist John Sandberg, first author of the article, says, "Contrary to popular belief, the increase in female labor force participation has not led to a decrease in the amount of time parents spend with their children. Even though parents, and especially mothers, may be busier than ever before, many seem to be managing to fit in more time with their children than an earlier generation of parents did."

The study, done with Michigan senior researcher Sandra Hofferth, was based on time diaries from two nationally representative samples of about 2,500 children.

Fathers appear to be taking up the slack in families where both parents are employed. While working mothers spend about five hours per week less time with children than at-home mothers, total parental time has increased. "This suggests that fathers may be taking more responsibility for child care when mothers work," Sandberg says.

The fact that overall time of parents with kids went up significantly over the past 20 years gives the lie to the notion that today's parents are so harried or otherwise absorbed that they slight their children. One intriguing fact to emerge from the study was that today's working mothers spend as much time with their children as did at-home mothers 20 years ago. In a more "traditional" time, mothers were spending less time with their kids. And the University of Maryland's Suzanne Bianchi found that mothers spend as much—if not more—time with their kids than mothers in 1965.[17] How do they do it? Less sleep, less housework, more time together when they're home. It's hard to make a case for a nation of selfish, absentee parents with these data.

And fathers are getting more involved with kids. National survey data show that men's time with kids is going up. Surveys at major corporations such as Du Pont and Merck show that men would sacrifice pay and promotions for more family time. Still, the news media persist in referring to the "decline of the family" as if it were a historical fact, and implying that the parents of yesteryear were just so much better than contemporary parents— which no evidence supports. As a journalist, I've encountered this issue personally. Once, after I had written an article about employed mothers, a woman called me on the phone to say that I had "abandoned" my children by working. I pointed out that, over the years, my husband and I have spent a lot of time with our kids. She was adamant about my terrible mothering, hinting darkly that my kids probably didn't turn out very well. I must remember to tell my federal-agent son and his wife and daughter and my Shakespearean actress daughter and her husband and two kids that they have a dim future, thanks to mom.

The idea that a woman can have no other "real" life once she is a mom was the subtext of a testy encounter in 2006 between actress Felicity Huffman (an Oscar nominee as well as a star of *Desperate Housewives)* and *60 Minutes'* Lesley Stahl.[18] When Stahl asked Huffman if motherhood wasn't the best thing in her life, the actress startled Stahl (and probably many viewers) by responding, "No. And I resent that question, because I think it puts women in an untenable position, because unless I say to you, 'Oh Lesley, it's the best thing I've ever done with my whole life,' I'm considered a bad mother. And just when I said no to you, you went back."

As journalist Mona Gable wrote on *The Huffington Post,* "Why do women always get asked the mommy question? Why is it assumed that for successful women, motherhood is the apotheosis of fulfillment? I don't even know if he has kids, but can you imagine Stahl asking Keanu Reeves that question? 'Excuse me, Keanu, but isn't fatherhood just the best?' Or say, Kiefer Sutherland from the hit show *24*? Ridiculous!"[19]

But women can't escape the "selfish" frame of the media, even if they have no children. An astonishing story in the *New York Times* in 2005 was headlined, "Forget the Career. My Parents Need Me at Home."[20] The lead anecdote was about a radio news anchor with a six-figure salary. The 49-year-old woman quit her job to live with her parents to care for a father with dementia and a depressed mother. The *Times* noted that she "sleeps in the dormered bedroom of her childhood and . . . starts her days reminding her father, Woody, a sweet-tempered 78-year-old who once owned an auto parts company, how to spoon cereal from his bowl. Then, in a Mercedes C230 that she calls the 'last remnant of my other life,' she takes him to adult day care, begging her mother to use her time alone to get a massage or take a painting class."

The woman said of herself, "I lived a very selfish life. I'd gotten plenty of recognition. But all I did was work, and it was getting old. I knew I could make a difference here."

The story continues approvingly about the "daughter" track, a modern version of the old custom that eldest daughters would never marry and instead devote their lives to caring for their parents. The *Times* continued, "Middle-aged women may see leaving a high-powered career as an opportunity, not a sacrifice, many experts say, which distinguishes the Daughter Track from the Mommy Track."

This story absolutely infuriated me. Having spent a brief time caring for an ailing parent (without quitting my job to do it, and hiring help), I know how incredibly difficult this sort of caregiving is. I wonder how soon the former radio newscaster, living in a cramped bedroom, with no income but a tiny stipend from her parents, dealing with a demented father day after day, will succumb to depression, burnout, and exhaustion. There is a veritable mountain of research about the psychic costs of such caregiving.

The fact that a story in a major paper would present the idea of single women leaving good jobs to return to full-time care of sick and aging parents as a terrific idea stunned me. Dismissing a lifetime of productive work as simply "selfishness" would never be done to—or by—a man. And nowhere in the story is there any dissenting voice to say, "Are you people nuts?" Returning to the nineteenth-century tradition of putting spinster ladies in charge of elder care is a *terrible* idea, a recipe for more, not fewer, psychiatric symptoms. The news frame here is not one of seeking sensible public policies for a huge national issue—elder care—but of bringing "selfish" women to their senses and back to their rightful places as caretakers of everybody else.

MOMMY VS. MOMMY

Everybody loves a catfight, none more so than the news media, so it's not surprising that The Mommy Wars have such staying power as a news frame. It was a staple of the early days of the women's movement, in which women were simplistically portrayed in the media either as aggressive harpies who wanted careers or sweet, docile stay-at-home wives. You'd think that, four decades later, this hackneyed notion would have faded from the media. Not so. Mommy Wars stories abound in the press. "Revisiting the Mommy Wars," headlined the *Christian Science Monitor* in 2001.[21] "New Salvo Is Fired in Mommy Wars," announced the *New York Times* in 2004.[22] *New York* magazine ran a 2002 cover piece titled "Who's the Better Mom?" based on the idea that at-work and at-home mothers were at war.[23] The article cited no statistics to document such a conflict, just a novel and a series of essays. In 2006, ABC aired a segment on *Good Morning America* that prompted NOW president Kim Gandy to protest, "From start to finish, this feature offered much heat but little light. The "Mommy Wars" title was the first clue that the story would pit one group of hard-working women against another."[24] It's the classic "fake trend" story. If you don't have any real facts, dredge up what you do have, feature a jazzy sound bite or cover picture (two mommies with jaws clenched), and top the confection off with a catchy headline. But is there any evidence for such a war? Very little. My daughter's generation— in their late twenties and early thirties—accept whatever roles their contemporaries choose. Sociologist Alan Wolfe, in his study of Americans and their values, found that, overall, Americans were very tolerant of other people's work and family life arrangements.[25]

What's really going on, says Stephanie Coontz, is the occasional *mommy spat.*[26] "There's an attempt by certain elements in our society to turn it into a war. But whatever its original reasons, it plays the function of allowing us to ignore the dilemmas facing all parents and all caregivers in society." The steady, continuing trend of women moving into the workforce is not going to reverse, and we need to examine how we can best care for infants, toddlers, young kids and teenagers. The promotion of ersatz mommy wars simply gets in the way of such a serious examination.

Ironically, publications aimed at women don't do a much better job on the mommy vs. mommy issue. A pair of professors from Hope College in Holland, Michigan, Deirdre Johnston and Debra Swanson, analyzed 20 issues of the most read traditional women's magazines (*Good Housekeeping* and *Family Circle*), parenting magazines (*Parents*), and the magazines with the highest composition of working mothers (*Working Mother* and *Family Fun*).[27] Overall, they found that the magazines promote a traditional motherhood ideology—with mom as white, middle class, educated, married, and at-home—but tend to present at-home mothers as unhappy and incompetent. "Depression is three to five times higher in mothers than in other populations," says Dr. Johnston. "These kinds of contradictory messages undermine a mother's instincts. It doesn't feel right to be told to do something and then be punished for it."

If I hear the phrase "You Can't Have It All" addressed to women (but never to men) one more time, I will shriek. Nobody ever has *all* of everything. But Having It All is code for a woman with both a family and a good job—which millions of women actually do have. They are not hassle free, they are sometimes stressed, they wish there were more hours in the day— but overall, they are doing well. The news media fail to grasp this fact. A perfect example is the *Time* cover story "The Case For Going Home,"[28] which first ran as the major feature in the magazine and then was repackaged for a *Time* special publication called the *Time A to Z Health Guide.*[29] The book may have more influence than the magazine, because it will not instantly disappear from newsstands.

The *Time* book begins its section on parenting this way: "Sorry, Mom, you can't have it all. Why more women are dropping out of the workplace to stay at home." The story continues, "Some 72 percent of mothers with children under 18 are in the workforce, compared with 45 percent who were working in 1975. But the numbers aren't rising."

Let's pause here for a moment. Do you notice a disconnect between the two paragraphs? The first says, "You can't have it all." But the second utterly contradicts that statement with the statistic showing that 72 percent actually do.

How often do you see a lead on a story that seems to have no connection with the numbers it offers? Would a political story about a candidate who had a 72 percent approval rating while his opponent had a 45 percent approval rating focus on the fact that the former's numbers were not rising? Or, take an issues story. If 72 percent of the population declared themselves in favor of prayer in schools while 45 percent were opposed, would the story suggest that school prayer advocates could not get their way? We are in the realm of Alice in Wonderland, where things just don't add up.

Clearly the real story of American women is that they are in the workforce in huge numbers and are likely to remain there, as the *Time* article concedes. Certainly, some women with young children are going home as they always have, but the major trend is holding steady. There may (or may not) be a slight uptick among women going home. *Time* admits, "because these women represent a small and privileged sector the dimensions of the exodus are hard to measure." Yet the article claims there is "A reluctant revolt" occurring among women in good jobs. But how can there be a "revolt" if the numbers are so tiny? It's an echo of the *New York Times Magazine* story called

"The Opt Out Revolution," which I dealt with in detail in chapter 1. (One wonders why the news media are so fascinated with the idea of privileged women going home. Is it because high-paid male media executives who make story decisions have wives who do just that?)

Having announced that women can't have it all, then promptly contradicting that statement with its own statistics, *Time* goes on to wax eloquent about the joys of staying home. "Despite misgivings, most women who step out of careers find unexpected delights on the home front, not to mention the enormous relief of no longer worrying about shortchanging the kids." The story then quotes from a book called *Maternal Desire: On Children, Love and the Inner Life* (2004), in which the author castigates feminists for "ignoring the basic urge felt by most mothers to spend meaningful time with their children."[30] (Here again, is the straw woman, the feminist who wants all women to work 70 hours a week, neglect their children while they dress for success, and care only about climbing the corporate ladder.) The book, says *Time,* "could prompt a thousand resignations." (Even though the article admits that the book puts an "idyllic gloss" on staying home.)

The entire section called "Parenting" in the book is devoted largely to at-home mothers, with only a few paragraphs toward the end dealing with issues faced by working mothers, such as family-friendly policies in the workplace. The news frame of the story features the roughly 22 percent of mothers who stay home rather than the 72–75 percent who work. Completely missing from the article is any notion that there could be a downside to full-time homemaking—despite the fact that, for years, research has been finding, as I noted in the previous chapter, that the traditional role offers a serious risk of depression and lack of self-esteem for women.

Isn't it irresponsible to fail to mention to women who are contemplating leaving work to stay home with their kids that these risks exist and to offer ways to avoid them? Won't women who find that being at home is not quite the delight that the media promised be more at risk? And more prone to feel like failures, since all the media mommies seem so deliriously happy?

The fact is that both women at work and women at home face problems and challenges, albeit not the same ones. Different women make different choices, based on their own desires, their financial resources and the needs of their children. Exaggerating the joys of at-home motherhood while dwelling on the frustrations of combining work and family serves women poorly. As does the reverse. Judith Warner's 2005 book *Perfect Madness: Motherhood in the Age of Anxiety* (subject of a *Newsweek* cover story) presents mothers so obsessed with producing perfect children, rushing from soccer practice to dance lessons to computer camps, that they are driving themselves crazy.[31] These, of course, are largely upper-middle-class mothers, and such women do exist, but are they typical? Are most at-home mothers driving themselves nuts trying to produce superchildren? Probably not. The book's saving grace is that it does point out the pressures on mothers, and the ways in which many women seem to think that, because they have chosen motherhood, they have no right to ask for any help. Warner rightly notes that this very American individualistic attitude can make women unlikely to use their political clout to push for such initiatives as early childhood education, better health care, or family-friendly policies in the workplace.

Women need informed, nonideological information on which to make life choices. But serious reporting of the issues involved would not be very sexy. Mommy Wars, Women Who Can't Have It All, phony revolutions, Dangerous Moms, and Crazy Moms make much better copy.

6
THE MUTED VOICE

Journalists, scholars, and others interested in public policy have noticed a growing silence: the absence of women's voices discussing serious issues in the nation's elite media. From op ed pages to brainy magazines to journals of opinion, women's voices are more muted than they have been in years. If the sound of men's opinions in the nation's media is a roar like Niagara, that of women's is the trickle of a bathroom faucet. On newspaper op ed pages and among the "talking heads" punditocracy, the fair sex gets an unfair shake.

This issue erupted in controversy in the spring of 2005 when USC law professor (and Fox News commentator) Susan Estrich offered her syndicated column to Michael Kinsley, then editorial page editor of the *Los Angeles Times*.[1] Things got nasty after the column was rejected, and Estrich pointed out the paucity of op eds written by women during Kinsley's tenure. She suggested his judgment might have been affected by his Parkinson's disease. Estrich apologized for that remark, but critics have used the incident to point out the glaring lack of women among media opinion makers.

The *Washington Post's* media columnist Howard Kurtz reported that in the two months before the Estrich complaint, 19.9 percent of op eds at the *LA Times* were by women, and the *Washington Post* clocked in at 10.4 percent.[2] He also noted that, among DC's talking heads, very few wear pantyhose.

As columnist Alicia Mundy writes in *Editor and Publisher,* at the *Washington Post,* "Op Ed pages are bulging with deep 'insider' pieces on foreign affairs to the near exclusion of more immediate issues. Second, these pages are almost entirely devoid of women." She notes that if you did a cursory search of the last two year's op ed pages, "You would be alarmed at the lack of diversity among writers and among subjects beyond foreign affairs."[3]

At the *New York Times,* the same situation prevails, despite the statements of editorial page editor Gail Collins that she wants more women's voices. Women writers grumble that they rarely even get a hearing at the *Times*. In 2005, Howard Kurtz noted that women were a mere 16. 9 percent of op ed writers in the *New York Times*.[4] That's roughly what I found during the month between November 4 and December 4 of 2002, when my own online search revealed that, of the nonregular columns on the op ed page, 60 were by men and 14 by women. (Three bylines featured names that were androgynous, so hard to identify.) Women also regularly get the "fluff" pieces. Two of the op eds by women could be called very light, one about the perfect Christmas gifts, another by Miss Manners on etiquette. When all op ed bylines were counted, of 92 writers, only 19 were women. (And, as of this writing, in 2006, the *Times* has seven male op ed columnists, plus Maureen Dowd.)

Even veteran women journalists have trouble getting heard these days. Mundy writes that Pulitzer Prize winner and syndicated columnist Ellen Goodman complained to her about getting bumped too often at the *Post*.[5] Geneva Overholser, the former Ombudsman at the *Post* and a respected editor and journalist, has been complaining for some time about the vanishing of women's voices on op ed pages and has noted the Post's "white male culture."[6]

Respected columnist Katha Pollitt (*The Nation*) made a similar complaint after the *Times*' Gail Collins said, "The pool of available people doing opinion writing is still tilted toward men. There are probably fewer women, in the great cosmic scheme of things, who feel comfortable writing very straight opinion stuff, and they're less comfortable hearing something on the news and batting something out."[7]

This infuriated Pollitt and many other experienced female journalists. As Pollitt rightly pointed out, "Feminine psychology doesn't explain why all five of *USA Today's* political columnists are male, or why *Time's* eleven columnists are male—down to the four in Arts and Entertainment—or why at *Newsweek* it's one out of six in print and two out of thirteen on the Web. According to *Editor and Publisher,* the proportion of female syndicated columnists (one in four) hasn't budged since 1999. The tiny universe of political-opinion writers includes plenty of women who hold their own with men, who do not wilt at the prospect of an angry e-mail, who have written cover stories and bestsellers and won prizes—and whose phone numbers are likely already in the Rolodexes of the editors who wonder where the women are."[8] Pollitt then went on to tick off a whole list of accomplished female pundits, and asked, "What am I, a potted plant?" to editors who just couldn't seem to find women.

If you read many op ed pages these days, you would think that issues of poverty, race, sexism, the health care crisis, working families, reproductive rights, and education had simply vanished from the planet. Mundy notes that at the *Post,* the op ed pages are "ploddingly predictable." She says, "most of the time they [columnists] gorge on what we women sarcastically used to call "Big ——— Issues (suggesting an excess of testosterone)."

On too many op ed pages, you find men writing the same thing over and over about Iraq, terrorism, and military questions, while room just can't be found for other issues. (Some papers, it should be said, manage to do better. From my own reading, I have found that *The Los Angeles Times* (before Kinsley's tenure) and the *Boston Globe,* for example, display both a wide range of issues and a respectable number of women writers.)

Do too many male editors (and some female ones) fail to resonate with pieces by women that reflect feminist viewpoints? Many critics say yes. A case in point, from *Chicago Sun Times* columnist Carol Slezak in April of 2005:[9]

> The magazine that gives us the annual swimsuit edition killed Martha Burk's commentary for purposes of taste. *Sports Illustrated* had invited Burk, chair of the National Council of Women's Organizations, to write a piece about the Augusta National controversy for publication in the current issue's "Golf Plus" section. (The club bars most female members.) Upon submitting her commentary, Burk received positive feedback from the magazine.
>
> "It definitely was going to run," Burk said, adding that SI asked her for a photograph to run with the piece, and also sent her a contract. But Burk's commentary didn't run, because managing editor Terry McDonell killed it.

Asked to explain, the editor said he found several of the author's comments objectionable, especially a reference to the Klu Klux Klan.

Slezak writes, "Asked why he didn't simply edit those parts he found objectionable, McDonell indicated he just didn't feel good about Burk's piece." Burk herself, reported Slezak, thought, "there might be more to SI's decision to kill her commentary. Was it motivated at least in part by fear of reprisal from corporate America? Ad sales drive publishing, after all, and Burk's piece mentions several big corporations by name. Perhaps someone didn't want to risk angering potential advertisers." When SI demurred, *Sporting News* decided to take the piece, but insisted that Burke remove the names of the corporate sponsors from the piece. She refused. End of story.

The situation seems to be getting worse. A spring 2005 report from the Project for Excellence in Journalism, which reviewed 17,000 news reports during 20 days in 2004, found that although women now make up more than half the US population and hold positions of power in government and business, their opinions are absent from large swaths of news coverage, particularly reports about politics, the military, and foreign policy.[10] Women were most likely to be included in feature stories about children, celebrities, and homemaking, among others.

Tom Rosenstiel, the project's director, said, "These numbers are really striking. I didn't expect that women would have made as little progress as these numbers seem to suggest in terms of becoming sources and being references in the news."

Reporters were more than three times as likely to cite two or more men within a news story as to cite a comparable number of women. The most male-dominated coverage was found in the sports pages and on some TV shows. MSNBC's *Hardball with Chris Matthews* had no female guests on three nights in April, May, and June; the sole female voice was that of a soldier's wife in a video clip about the prisoner abuse scandal in Iraq. Rosenstiel said "a broader, fuller and more accurate account of who we are as a society requires that there be more women in the news because they play a bigger role in the culture."

NO EXPERTS HERE

On TV news, women emerge much more often as ordinary citizens, crime victims, or subjects of "soft" feature stories than they do as authoritative voices. A 2001 study by Media Tenor Ltd., a nonpartisan German media analysis group with offices in New York, studied the content of the ABC, CBS, and NBC evening news shows.[11] Women made up only 9 percent of professional and political voices. More than half the women who appeared on the news (52 percent) were presented as "ordinary citizens," while only 14 percent of the men who appeared were in this category. Women, it seems, are people that events happen to, but they do not comment upon or control them. A paltry 0.2 percent of coverage was of gender issues, but even then, the study found, women weren't the experts. Women were presented as non-expert citizens 77 percent of the time in gender stories, while men spoke in these stories as experts *100 percent* of the time. By 2004, the story was the same. A study by the Women's Funding Network showed that Women were also less likely to make repeat appearances on these programs and tended to appear in later segments of the programs.[12]

At the most respected magazines and journals in the nation, the situation is no better. Look at *The New Yorker, Harpers, The Atlantic, The New York Times Magazine*—once again, you will see few female bylines. When Ruth Davis Konigsberg, a deputy editor at *Glamour*, started counting them in 2005, she tallied 324 males writing, and 99 females in *Harpers, The New Yorker, The New York Times Magazine,* and *Vanity Fair.*[13] The *Columbia Journalism Review* reported that in an analysis of 11 magazines published between October 2003 and May 2005, male-to-female byline ratios ranged from 13:1 at the *National Review* to 7:1 at *Harper's* and *The Weekly Standard* to 2:1 at the *Columbia Journalism Review.*[14]

But the situation is even worse than it looks at first glance, because the men usually get the big feature stories while the women most often pen back-of-the book features, book reviews, etc. In 2005–06, four major intellectual magazines—the *Atlantic,* the *New Republic,* the *Paris Review,* and *Harper's*—appointed new editors-in-chief—all men. Asked what the four have in common, the *New Republic's* Franklin Foer replied, "White guys are still in charge."[15]

At the *Atlantic,* there exists what might be called a journalistic apartheid where women are concerned. If you're a regular reader of the publication, which I am, you'd think that some sort of plague had decimated the female population. Women barely exist in the *Atlantic's* worldview. Typical is the April 2005 issue, which features articles on Fighting China, Saddam's legal case, Geraldo Rivera, and a French male journalist's view of America. Women get mentioned only in a tongue-in-cheek review of a series of parenting books by humorist Sandra Tsing Loh.[16] The June 2006 issue featured 18 articles by men on such heavy issues as the Iraq war, education, abortion politics, and American management, and four by women—one on domestic help, another about being a New Yorker, two book reviews, and a regular feature on writing.[17] Between December 2001 and December 2002, I did a count and found 38 major articles by men and 7 by women. Two of these women were writing with their more famous husbands; another was doing an anecdotal piece on cross-dressing. So, for serious pieces, the total is 38 to 4. The essays were even worse. During this period, I found 41 essays by men, and 2 by women. Or to be precise, 2 essays by the *same* woman. For the *Atlantic,* Margaret Talbot represented all of womanhood.

Atlantic also regularly trashes feminism. In recent years, it used its cover to feature two articles very critical of feminists. One was an excerpt from Christina Hoff Sommers's *The War Against Boys*[18] and in 2004 a tirade by Caitlin Flanagan titled "How Serfdom Saved the Women's Movement"[19] charging that feminists advanced their cause on the back of cheap domestic labor by poor women of color.

The article was utterly simplistic, reducing feminism to a bunch of rich white women who wanted prestige jobs, and failing to note that many businesses owned by white men are built on the backs of poor minority workers. And an astonishing book review[20] in 2005 of the new edition of *Our Bodies, Ourselves for the New Century*[21] proclaimed that women "have more to fear from other women than from men." The bulk of the review, written by a woman, prattled on about the book's alleged "attack on beauty" and included this whopper: "It is not freedom from beauty that needs defending, but freedom *for* beauty." (To the barricades for Paris Hilton, Anna Nicole Smith, and Angelina Jolie, poor wretches?)

If *Atlantic* was the only publication you read, you would learn that feminism was an evil movement that aimed to destroy men and boys and people of color and to insist that women wear only sackcloth and ashes. And in 2005, the magazine ran a piece called "Letting Go of Roe," in which the author calls the Supreme Court decision making abortion legal "a doctrinally indefensible court decision."[22]

At the *New Yorker,* things are only a bit better. On the website MobyLives, Dennis Loy Johnson points out that while many—perhaps most—*New Yorker* readers are female, few of the magazine's bylines are.[23] He said he was tipped off to this fact by a senior publishing executive, and decided to make his own count at the New York Public Library. He found that 80 percent of the writing in the magazine at that point (the summer of 2002) was by men. Even worse, "The overwhelming majority of writing contributed by women was written by staffers and appeared in the magazine's back pages." He notes that the woman who had published the most poetry in the magazine at that time was Dana Goodyear, editor-in-chief David Remnick's 25-year-old assistant." Ruth Davis Konigsberg found the byline gap to be 98 men to 27 women in 2005. The same situation held at the *New York Times Magazine* (103 to 36). The highly influential *New York Times Book Review* is also a male bastion. A study by Brown University professor Paula Caplan found that in 53 issues of the review, 72 percent of all books reviewed were written by men and 66 percent of those reviews carried male bylines.[24]

Young female journalists who want to work for magazines often find themselves steered toward fashion and food writing and away from the "serious" publications that gobble up the young white guys. I've heard them complain (in blogs and in person) that they find it hard to get onto the track that leads to punditry and prestige. Young men with less experience pass them by in the realm of "serious" journalism.

The situation is no less dire for women scholars and journalists who want to influence the public agenda of the nation. I haven't seen such a dearth of women's voices since the premovement days when women were completely invisible in the media. And in journalism, the number of women gatekeepers is on the wane. Just one in five of top female newspaper editors expect to stay where they are, because they see no road to the top. One in two expect to leave their company or the news business entirely, according to a major 2002 report by the American Press Institute and the Pew Center for Civic Journalism.[25] A report from the media management center at Northwestern in 2002 found few women in top newspaper jobs.[26] "Few opportunities exist for women to make it to the top," the report concluded. While women hold 44 percent of newspaper jobs, tiny numbers of them are in the executive suite. Women have in fact lost ground, dropping from 29 percent of executive jobs in 2000 to 26 percent in 2002. Eighty-six percent of top jobs in newspapers were held by men, the report noted. Surveys showed these trends persisting in 2005.[27] As Northwestern journalism professor Michele Weldon notes, "Something goes awry between studying for journalism and working in it."[28] She reports that women represent more than 70 percent of students in journalism schools but, "In the newsrooms, the number is half that." In newsrooms, in 2005, 65.2 percent of all supervisors were men. They were also 58.8 percent of all copy editors, 60.1 percent of reporters, and 72.6 percent of photographers.[29]

In the internet and telecommunications industries, a 2002 study by the Annenberg Foundation found that women hold only 16 percent of executive jobs in telecommunications and 18 percent in Internet companies.[30] Are "new media" becoming a boys club, as the old media were for so long (and may become once again)? The following year, Annenberg reported "no progress" for women in "breaking the glass ceiling. In fact, fewer than one in five board members of the nation's largest communications companies are women. Only 10 of the 57 companies surveyed had women board members. And only a paltry 5 percent of women executives had what the report called "clout" titles (senior vice president through chief executive officer).[31]

The money trend line is just as dismal among journalists reporting for newsmagazines, radio, newspapers, television, and wire services. The *American Journalist* survey released in April 2003 showed that female journalists' median salary in 2001 was $37,731, about 81 percent of men's median salary of $46,758, the same percentage as in 1991.[32]

Media content is shaped largely by men. As noted earlier, a paltry 14 percent of guests on the Sunday morning talk shows in 2004 were women, No pantyhose here, as Howard Kurtz observed.[33] Talk radio is completely dominated by right-wing males, most with the attitude of Rush Limbaugh about women as Feminazis. (Liberal radio is trying, but has nowhere near the market share of the conservatives.) On cable TV, there are no opinionated talk show hosts like Bill O'Reilly, Sean Hannity, Joe Scarborough, etc. who are women. The women who host cable talk shows usually take the reporter role, like Paula Zahn. They may sometimes ask probing questions but rarely offer political opinions. The one avowedly pro-feminist host was Phil Donahue, who quickly disappeared. Some women guests are brought on to offer opinions, but they are often fodder for conservatives whose main function appears to be to start a screaming match.

What's to be done about this state of affairs? Studies and reports and complaints don't seem to have helped. The silence has only deepened. Some advocate that women should move out of the mainstream and into the blogosphere to be heard, but so far that's not much of an economic strategy. The mainstream media are still the 800-pound gorilla. A 2003 report by the International Newspaper Marketing Association found that newspapers do a poor job of reaching out to women, still producing male-oriented products.[34] "Even newspapers already pursuing the lucrative female market with specific sections or supplements tend to base their efforts on myths, stereotypes, and anecdotal evidence instead of hard data." The world is still seen as a male arena. Instead of "bringing more of the content that interests women forward onto Page One, newspapers have instead tended to throw women a bone in the form of women's sections or periodic female-themed supplements."

Maybe women readers, viewers, and listeners hold the key. Maybe they ought to simply stop buying publications that rarely cover their issues and seem to hold women writers in contempt. Money talks, and it's time women used the power of their pocketbooks.

The internet may be a prime vehicle to do just that. In August of '06, Forbes.com ran a column by editor Michael Noer titled "Don't Marry Career Women."[35] It claimed that research proves that men who wed professional women are unhappy. The story—perhaps designed to create "buzz"— was a sinkhole of bad science and misunderstood data.

What happened? Women bloggers were outraged and said so all over the web. Forbes.com quickly took down the story and ultimately, publisher Steve Forbes had to apologize for insulting working women. It was a major story on the ABC evening news.

For once, the Spiral of Silence was shattered.

7 HATING HILLARY, TRASHING TERESA, AND MAULING MARTHA

"Is there a more reviled public figure in America today than Hillary Rodham Clinton?" asked *Boston Phoenix* media critic Dan Kennedy in June of 2005.[1] He noted, "In the large and growing class of politicians thinking about running for president, the junior senator from New York is surely the most controversial and—yes—the most despised."

The American news media are partly to blame for this state of affairs, because they too often channel the well-financed ire of the right-wing activists who have made a cottage industry out of hating Hillary. Giving lots of ink to even the most ludicrous charges insures that some of the mud will stick. In June of 2006, conservative critic John Podhoretz tried to terrify the right wing with a book called *Can She Be Stopped? Hillary Clinton Will Be the Next President of the United States Unless . . .*[2] What the news media picked up on was the author's statement that Senator Clinton was "pathologically unsexy . . . not a raving beauty." And he used the "B" word. Often. "Just for vulgarity's sake, let me put it this way. She's got to be a bitch [to win]. And Hillary is a bitch."

Even worse was a 2005 book by Ed Klein, a former *New York Times* journalist turned celebrity hound: *The Truth About Hillary: What She Knew, When She Knew It and How Far She'll Go to Become President.*[3] Most reviewers admitted it was poorly sourced, reliant on rumor, and filled with ludicrous charges. Guess what? It immediately became a bestseller, zooming to number two on the *Times* bestseller list days after it was published.

Perhaps the nuttiest of Klein's charges was a suggestion that Chelsea Clinton was the product of marital rape, which was featured on the infamous Matt Drudge website.[4] Klein alleges that an unnamed friend of Bill and Hillary, who was with them on a trip to Bermuda in 1979, heard Bill remark, "Now I'm gong to go home and rape my wife." Klein then uses an anonymous source to say that, in the morning, the Clintons' room "looked like World War III. There were pillows and busted-up furniture all over the place." Shortly afterward, Hillary announced that she was pregnant.

In addition to the salacious "rape" story, Klein suggested that Hillary—despite being a married woman with a child, was a lesbian. In an interview with conservative talk show host Sean Hannity, Klein said that Hillary had "given all kinds of signals that her sexuality is in question."[5] He cited no evidence, just lots of innuendo.

Tina Brown, Klein's former editor at *Vanity Fair,* pointed out in the *Washington Post,* "Every time Klein describes anyone female in Hillary Clinton's circle, you hear the clump clump clump of stereotype-lesbian footwear. Melanne Verveer, her White House east wing chief of staff is 'dark-haired and mannish looking.' [Aide] Susan Thomases has 'frizzy salt and pepper hair, frumpy clothes, down at the heels shoes and an expletive-laden vocabulary' and Evelyn Lieberman, the White House deputy Chief of Staff is 'short, a little overweight with grayish hair.'"[6]

Brown notes that even when Hillary makes a joke at a Wellesley reunion about the buzz cut of a lesbian classmate and laughs that maybe she too should get a cut like that, Klein sees the lavender menace. He suggests that her remark was "A hint of wishful thinking," instead of what it obviously was, a clear tease off the media's obsession with her hair.

The week the book appeared, I found more than fifty media stories about it, some in newspapers as far away as Australia. Astonishingly, according to Google, the book was mentioned on 1,210,000 pages on the web.

Once upon a time, such a book—dismissed as trash even by many conservatives, including Peggy Noonan and Bill O'Reilly—would have died a merciful death. But the infotainment tsunami that is present-day media guaranteed that the book would be read and talked about. As a *New York Times* story about the book noted, "there is no such thing as bad publicity, and even criticisms of the book that repeat its more salacious charges about Mrs. Clinton's personal and marital life could help its sales."[7] That's what hard-right conservatives hoped. The book was published by Sentinel, a new conservative imprint of Penguin, and heavily promoted by Newsmax.com, a site partially bankrolled by millionaire Richard Mellon Scaife, who financed investigations of the Clintons in the 1990s. And a slew of right-wing websites explicitly promised to "Swift-Boat" Senator Clinton—referring to the very effective campaign against John Kerry in the 2004 election.[8]

Hillary Clinton has long been a lightning rod for the media. Consider the attacks on her during Bill's first campaign, when she was called cold, calculating, and way too ambitious. According to the *New York Times,* Hillary Clinton was in fact likened to the infamous Mrs. Macbeth no fewer than 20 times in major articles in 1992, with "witch" references to her coming in a strong second.[9] She was also compared to the murderess played by Glenn Close in the movie *Fatal Attraction*. Following the release of her memoir *Living History* in 2004, Hillary again came under media attack, with some critics claiming the book was total fiction and others accusing her of upstaging democratic presidential nominees to highlight her own star power.[10] At that time, the episode made me wonder what high-profile female in the political ring would next be singled out for demonizing. The answer came quickly: Teresa Heinz Kerry, philanthropist, environmentalist, and the millionaire wife of presidential candidate John Kerry.

In a press pile-on in 2004, she emerged as peculiar, eccentric, and vain, with an emphasis on her botox injections and prenup agreement. After she gave a candid interview to *Elle* magazine, the national press dug through the story and seemed to decide—as a group—that she should pipe down. An item about the interview in the *Washington Post* was headlined "The Ungagable Teresa Heinz."[11] The *New York Post* followed with the headline "Salty Tongue," topping its story about the *Elle* interview.[12] The *Boston Globe* ran an op ed column saying she "talks at excruciating length, in an excruciatingly dirge-like voice, on any number of topics."[13] *Newsweek*'s cover story asked, "Loose Cannon—Or Crazy Like a Fox?"[14]

Whether Teresa should shut up was topic "A" on the cable news shows for a time. Whether one tuned to Fox or MSNBC or CNN, the chatter was about her reaction to Richard Nixon's 1992 comment that an outspoken wife would not be good for a candidate. She was slapped down for saying, "Well, we know Richard Nixon wasn't too much in contact with what women should be." In the *New York Times*, John Tierney accused her of "casually insulting a dead president and first lady."[15] Even columnist Maureen Dowd jumped on the bandwagon, saying that John Edwards's adoring gaze at John Kerry was taking the place of the one he *wasn't* getting from Teresa.[16] "Heaven knows Teresa was never going to do it," Dowd decreed. "Her attention rarely seems to light on her husband when she's at a microphone with him." Dowd added, "She doesn't gaze like Nancy or glare like Lee Hart or look appraisingly at her husband like Elizabeth Edwards. She doesn't always seem to notice he's there. When Mr. Kerry moves in for a nuzzle or a kiss, she sometimes makes a little face . . . She siphons attention from a husband who has a hard enough time getting it."

When Heinz Kerry told a reporter from a right-wing publication that had consistently attacked her to "shove it," you'd have thought she had decreed "Off with his head!" The *Atlanta Journal* chided her "rash pronouncements" and called her a mixed blessing to her husband.[17] "Money to Burn—and a

Mouth to Fan the Flames," headlined the *London Telegraph*.[18] The *Seattle Times* brayed, "Putting a Lid on the Loose Lips of Teresa Heinz Kerry."[19]

So Heinz Kerry is vain, blabby, and not kissy-kissy enough with her husband, the media decree. But if the "T" in her first name stood for Tom instead of Teresa, would we be getting a different spin? Would we be hearing about a world-class philanthropist who runs the Washington-based Heinz foundations, who endowed two environmental chairs at Harvard and created programs to deal with the expenses of prescription drugs and the problems women face in retirement? Do we ever hear that billionaire philanthropist George Soros talks too much? Do we hear about what medications Bill Gates takes? Do we know if either of these men has personal tics, and do we worry about their abs or their wardrobes? Teresa Heinz Kerry is European and does not behave in the docile manner the American media expect of political women. Her family is from Portugal and she herself grew up in Mozambique. She is an intellectual who speaks five languages and has serious commitments to a number of weighty issues. Her foundation developed a model prescription drug plan for senior citizens. She oversees scholarships for minority students who study science. She serves on a number of corporate and university boards. She created the H. John Heinz III Center for Science, Economics and the Environment in Washington, named for her late first husband. She certainly did not fit the outmoded stereotype of the ideal first lady, who smiles, says little, and concerns herself with the floral arrangements. I have heard her speak about environmental issues with passion and knowledge. That didn't count much with the national media.

Ironically, while the news media often presented Teresa Heinz Kerry as tough and mannish, her war-hero husband was pictured as wavering, indecisive, foppish, and rather unmanly—despite the fact that he steered his swift boat right into enemy fire during the Vietnam War. In the primaries, another democratic candidate, Howard Dean, became an irrational (dare we say *feminized*) hysteric in the eyes of the media. In a crowded hall in Iowa, he declared he was going to carry his campaign to other states, and in a manner appropriate for a hall packed with adoring political supporters, he uttered a holler aimed at the rafters. The problem was, of course, that in the translation from the "hot" medium of the political hall to the "cool" medium of television, Dean was transformed from the cool, rational doctor to the uncontrollable hysteric.[20] As for his physician wife, the news media simply could not comprehend a woman who vowed to stay at her job and not move to Washington, and who practiced medicine under her maiden name, Judith Steinberg. As Joan Vennochi observed in the *Boston Globe,* "America's voters still want a wife at a candidate's side, not a physician at her patient's side."[21] But if the news media hadn't found her so odd, maybe voters would not have either.

In fact, it's almost impossible for first-lady candidates to impress the media. Eleanor Roosevelt was cruelly maligned by political enemies for everything from her activism to her clothes to her slightly protruding teeth. Kitty Dukakis was dubbed a "Dragon Lady," Rosalynn Carter was the "Steel Magnolia," Barbara Bush was criticized for her weight, Nancy Reagan got nailed for seeing an astrologer and encouraging her husband to negotiate with the Russians.

HAIL TO THE CHIEF?

How long will it be before a woman hears this presidential ditty played for her? Probably a good while—and the media are a key player in this slow climb to the top. There is a double standard of accomplishment for men and women. Men step easily from different walks of life into a run for the top job. Women don't.

Ross Perot left private business to make a serious bid for the US presidency, as did Steve Forbes. Ralph Nader drew on his years as an anti-corporate activist to mount a presidential campaign that drew millions of voters. Ronald Reagan used his visibility as an actor and president of the Screen Actors Guild to vault into politics. General Colin Powell could have had the republican nomination if he'd wanted it in 2000.

But could women do the same? Will Condoleezza Rice ever appear on the head of a ticket? Could feminist Gloria Steinem or conservative activists Linda Chavez or Lynn Cheney have leapt from activism to presidential politics? What about Oprah Winfrey, not only one of the world's most successful entrepreneurs, but a famous talk show host as well? Or could actor-activist Susan Sarandon make a successful leap into top-level politics as California governor Arnold Schwarzenegger did?

You would be hard pressed to find a political pundit who would give any one of these women a snowball's chance in you-know-where. There may be only one job that could produce a female president: governor of a state.

Women, despite all the gains they have made, are rarely seen by the news media as effective leaders and managers. Philanthropist Barbara Lee, one of the founders of the White House Project (aimed at getting a woman in the White House), sees the governor's mansion as the best launching pad for a future chief executive.[22] Her foundation conducted a multi-part study of women running for governor, which resulted in a guide called *Keys to the Governor's Office*.[23]

Women candidates interviewed were well aware of the barriers they faced. One said, "Even though everybody knew my credentials were vastly superior to my opponent's, a woman can't do it. It is the feeling—and I've had this every time I've run for office—that 'I just can't picture myself walking into the governor's office and having to deal with a woman.'"

Women still start out in back of the pack in most races—no matter what their credentials. Elizabeth Dole is a good example. She seemed superbly positioned, in 2000, to make a strong run for the presidency. Many men would have given their eyeteeth for her credentials: former cabinet member in the Reagan administration, head of a well-known national organization (the Red Cross), high name recognition. More important, in poll after poll, she beat Al Gore head-to-head when voters were asked what presidential candidate they would prefer.

But researchers Caroline Headman, Susan J. Carroll, and Stephanie Olson of Rutgers University note that, early on, while political insiders and the public regarded Dole as a strong contender, the media did not.[24] The three presented their study of the coverage of Dole's candidacy at a meeting of the American Political Science Association.

Once a darling of the press, Dole seemed to visibly shrink in media accounts the more serious she became. Before she ran for president, it was hard to find an article that didn't present Dole as accomplished, capable, and charming. Suddenly, Liddy Dole turned into the Wicked Witch of the West, overambitious, chilly, and nasty under the "syrupy" Southern accent. Here's *Time* describing her with her staff: "If a staff member is lax, the unlucky individual gets the LOOK—set jaw, icy stare—and is frozen out." If a man presented this visage to his staff, he'd be seen as a forceful, take-charge personality.

Early on, the Rutgers scientists report, Dole was never covered the same way her male colleagues were. She never got the level of coverage that her polling indicates she should have had. In fact, she received about the same coverage as Gary Bauer and Steve Forbes, two decidedly uncharismatic men who lacked polling strength and had little chance of winning. In most respects, Dole's coverage was similar to that of Forbes, Bauer, and outsider Alan Keyes. George W. Bush and John McCain received much more coverage.

Often, the press focused on Dole's "first woman" status, giving the impression that she was a "backbencher," not the seasoned political operative she in fact was. In preprimary days, the study found, John McCain received quite favorable attention, even when he was only a relatively unknown face in the crowd and well before he became a media star. He was often called a "presidential hopeful," while Dole was usually mentioned in terms of her presumed inability to raise money. "Dole was most often described as a candidate lacking fund-raising ability and a real shot at the nomination." Of course this became self-fulfilling prophecy. The more the press says you can't raise money, the more you can't raise money.

The press focused more on Dole's personality traits than those of other candidates. She was called "rehearsed, scripted, robotic, controlled, frozen, a Stepford Wife." (Could these same qualities in a man be called "focused, stays on message, articulate?") Her speaking style was dubbed "Tammy Faye Bakker meets the Home Shopping Network." There was speculation about her sex life, and her hairdo was compared to an immobile fabric that wouldn't wrinkle or stretch.

Also, the press often portrayed her as a lightweight. "Dole's character and her substance were questioned to such a degree and in such critical ways that it is hard to imagine that gender biases were not at play," write the Rutgers political scientists.

Dole indeed had some real problems—including her husband, former Senator Robert Dole, whose careless comments about preferring another candidate to his wife made her look silly. But male candidates' perceived deficiencies do not cause the media to write them off. In 2000, George W. Bush's malapropisms and his lack of knowledge about the world were lampooned in late-night comedy, and in the robotic department, Al Gore made Liddy Dole look positively spontaneous. These were not seen as serious impediments to their quest for the presidency.

All this points out why the governorship may be the only credible route of the first woman president. First of all, the job trumps women's perceived incompetence and lack of experience. If you can run a state, it's hard for people to say you can't be a leader, or that you are a political novice. (Even if you are in the Senate, you will face the charge that you can't manage people or meet a payroll.)

The Lee Foundation study had some good news and some bad news for these candidates. Across the board, men prefer male candidates, while women are often undecided. Voters over 50 strongly prefer men—but younger, college-educated women express a strong preference for female candidates. Suburban voters tend to be fiscally conservative and socially moderate, with an open mind about gender. It may be that the first woman who hears "Hail to the Chief" when she enters a room will be a college-educated, centrist soccer mom who has paid her dues by spending a lot of time in the governor's mansion.

"Power: Do Women Really Want It?" was the headline on the cover of *For-*

tune in 2003.[25] I can't imagine that being written about a man. In other nations, women are routinely advancing to top positions in politics and in business. Michelle Bachelet was elected president of Chile and Patricia Russo became head of a telecom giant (a merger of Alcatel and Lucent, based in France) that will be one of the largest companies in the world. Angela Merkel serves as chancellor of Germany. Ellen Johnson-Sirleaf was elected president of Liberia.

Meanwhile, in the United States, we're still arguing over whether women have "the right stuff" to be leaders. Harvard political science professor Harvey Mansfield, in a 2006 book (*Manliness*) that got substantial media attention, claimed there has been only one real woman leader—Margaret Thatcher.[26] Teaching other women to be assertive, Mansfield wrote, might be "like teaching a cat to bark."

Powerful women in this country are always regarded with great suspicion, and if they get in trouble, they are often treated more harshly than men who misbehave. Take, for example, Martha Stewart, the homemaking guru who went to prison for using insider information to make a stock trade.

I wonder if Martha Stewart is rather like Eve—taking the rap for male bad behavior? It was Adam who ate the apple, after all, but it's Eve who still gets blamed for getting us thrown out of paradise. Or is she the new Leona Helmsley—the woman in business who falls from grace and gets all the brickbats, while the male miscreants slither away?

The female face of bad behavior gets more press than the male one. Martha Stewart was convicted for dumping stock on an insider tip. She was a good buddy of Sam Waksal, the CEO of ImClone. When he learned that the FDA was not going to approve his company's cancer drug, he ditched his own stocks and reportedly clued in his pal.

If true, it's an illegal act, but one that seems, in the light of recent scandals, relatively harmless to others. (Except, of course, those who hold stock in Martha's company, which plunged, but recovered.) Ken Lay and Jeff Skilling sold their stocks in Enron for millions, while their employees were forbidden to sell *their* stock in the doomed company. Thousands of employees lost their entire pension savings—dreams were broken, lives wrecked. As of this writing, Lay and Skilling have been convicted. Lay died of a heart attack, while Skilling is free on appeal. WorldCom CEO Bernard Ebbers was convicted of helping put together an $11 billion accounting fraud, but few Americans know his name.

Analyst Jack Grubman of Salomon Smith Barney was pushing WorldCom even as it sank. There are allegations that he was way too close to the companies whose stocks he was pushing, and that his firm made millions from business deals with them. He gets to retire with twenty million dollars.

But it's Martha Stewart who got most of the ink, most of the time.

If I had a conspiratorial mind, I'd wonder whether Stewart was set up as the perfect diversion. The media pack howled after her, talk shows wanted to book her, the Congress wanted to grill her. Meanwhile, the conflict-of-interest legislation that passed the Congress was a pallid pill, not really dealing with many major abuses. Business as usual went on for the big boys, while the public was allowed to vent its rage at Stewart—who, despite her fame, is really a minor cog in the great wheel of American capitalism.

In the last great American business scandal, the insider trading of the eighties, some big players went to jail, but the most hated icon of the business world was another minor female figure, the afore-mentioned Leona Helmsley. The hotel magnate wrote off the swimming pool and some of the furniture at her estate as business, rather than personal, expenses to the tune of $1.7 million. Not exactly up there in the annals of corporate crime with Harding's Teapot Dome scandal, but Leona got the full media treatment. She made the fatal mistake of saying, "Only the Little People pay taxes." (She denies she said it, but a housekeeper said she did, and the quote is now part of legend.)[27] She was dubbed "The Queen of Mean" on magazine covers for her treatment of the hired help. A *Newsweek* cover story about her headlined "Rhymes with Rich."[28] She served 18 months in prison and paid $6.3 million in fines.

In contrast, junk bond king Michael Milken, who pled guilty to six counts of security fraud, served two years in prison—barely more than Leona. He has, since his release, devoted his time to good works in education and health.

As for Martha Stewart, her problem is, of course, that she sells perfection—and everybody loves to see a Miss Perfect get her comeuppance. I have no great affection for Stewart, because she peddles the idea that every woman can achieve the sort of household and cuisine that Victorian ladies were able to manage only with a household of servants. Stewart makes every busy working mom feel inferior.

But still, there was real danger in making Martha the big story of business crime. The more the TV spots and the news stories and the magazine covers focused on her, the more the public's attention was drawn away from practices that have become standard operating procedure in too many executive suites. While we figuratively stoned Martha Stewart, and actually sent her to jail, the real swindlers faded into obscurity, often getting to keep their mansions and their ill-gotten gains from stock options. Some of them will probably pop up running companies again.

So if you were chortling over Martha Stewart's fate because your soufflés fall, your flowers wilt, and you can barely sew a button on, it was OK to enjoy the moment. But we shouldn't be so distracted that we let the big fish keep on swimming away, and let *same-old same-old* be the order of the day in corporate America.

Second Acts?

What's interesting, though, is that, as I was following the saga of Martha Stewart, the story took an unexpected lurch. Today, we may not, in fact, be pitying the diva of domesticity—we may be back to envying her. Who says there are no second acts in American life? Stewart, it seems, emerged from her stay in the prison dubbed Camp Cupcake as a reborn woman, one who scrubbed toilets without complaint and bonded with her less fortunate cellmates. Maybe it was just good PR, but Martha came out of prison with her image softened, and her perfection dimmed. *USA Today* noted in 2005, "It seems that since Martha Stewart emerged from her five-month sojourn behind bars, there has been a change in the billionaire's famously aloof demeanor. The new version dispenses smiles and hugs with abandon, is refocusing her magazine on the emotional 'whys' of homemaking and rails passionately against mandatory-minimum prison sentences. Mostly, she's just uncharacteristically cuddly, from her prison-made poncho to her emotional hellos."[29] A *Newsweek* cover headlined *Martha's Last Laugh* pictures her smiling broadly.[30] "What a difference a prison stay makes," the magazine gushes. "When Martha Stewart, 63, walks out of jail, most likely this Friday, America will be ready to embrace a reformed woman. No longer is she the poster child of bad behavior who's just getting her just desserts." Stewart's Anglo-Saxon blonde good looks and her PR-savvy friends probably didn't hurt her in this regard. As of this writing, she's had her own TV reality show, her company's stock price is climbing, and she may emerge more successful than ever.

Not so Leona Helmsley. Although she went back to running the hotel chain her husband founded, she will be forever reviled as The Queen of Mean in the media and the popular mind. There was even a TV movie of that name. Her own lawyers called her "A notorious, widely reviled, vastly wealthy new York Jew" to try to keep her out of prison by presenting media bias against her.[31] When she was sprung, there was no talk of a new Leona, no media stories that I could discover about her life in prison, no one seemed curious about what she made of prison life. If she "reformed," no one knew about it. She stayed notorious and widely reviled. And, of course, remained a New York Jew.

For some women, it seems, there are no second acts.

8
LADIES OF THE RIGHT

She's miniskirted, bottle-blonde, and mean as a warthog. The news media just adore her.

Ann Coulter is one of the new breed of female media pundits who find trash-talking about women to be a more-than-gainful means of employment. You see them all over the cable shows, the right-wing women who claim that feminism destroyed everything, and who far outnumber feminists when it comes to the talking heads of cableland, and on op ed pages as well. The news media can't get enough of these women. Bash feminism, and instantly you get calls from all the cable shows, the network producers, and the life-style sections of newspapers just panting to interview you about how miser-able women are today and how wonderful it used to be.

Ann Coulter has become a one-woman publishing industry, churning out bestseller after bestseller, in part because, as David Carr noted in the *New York Times,* "No other author in American publishing is better at weaponiz-ing words."[1] If Ann Coulter didn't exist, someone would have to invent her. She's the perfect creature for the ethereal planet of Infotainment, a realm where fact hardly exists, compassion is a yawn, civility a bore, and the na-tional anthem is "Another opening, another show." She is the perfect icon of the way in which the values of show business now have almost completely taken over what we used to call news and comment.

In June of 2006, as her latest book about liberals (*Godless: The Church of Liberalism*)[2] was to roll off the presses, Coulter took out after the outspoken 911 widows, to wit: "These broads are millionaires, lionized on TV and in articles about them, reveling in their status as celebrities and stalked by grief-arazzis. I have never seen people enjoying their husband's death so much."[3] She also called them "harpies," whose husbands were probably about to divorce them before the towers fell.

Coulter's comments on the widows were everywhere on planet Infotain-ment in the spring of 2006, but it's sometimes hard to figure out whether she's a spoof segment on the *Daily Show,* a sitcom character too caricatured to exist in the world that isn't composed of electrons dashing to and fro, or a latter-day Father Coughlin who spreads hate like hair spray.

Were her vitriolic comments a slip of the lip, a gaffe to be regretted, perhaps? Not at all. As the *Times* noted, "That doozy of a sentence was written, edited, lawyered and then published. By now, she, along with Crown Publishing, have come up with a dexterous formula for kicking up the kind of fuss that sells books."[4]

The book world, alas, has been sucked into the black hole of planet Infotainment. What used to be the realm of Emerson, Faulkner, and Wolfe is now chockfull of packaged plagiarism, celebrity trivia, and wall-to-wall gossip, diet, and advice.

Coulter's newest book once again takes on her favorite bete noir, liberals. In *Godless* she says they will burn in hell for casual sex, for opposing school prayer, not believing that the world was created in six days, and not thinking sex ed is the handiwork of Satan. In her last book, *Treason: Liberal Treachery from the Cold War to the War on Terrorism,* Joe McCarthy was the good guy and all democrats, she said, ought be to hanged as anti-American Benedict Arnolds.[5]

She'd positively hate to hear this, but ironically, Ann Coulter is a feminist success story. She's a lawyer who has an opinion every 3.4 seconds and gets paid very well for them. She's a sought-after guest on talk shows, her lecture fees are spectacular, and she's become a media megastar.

Back in the 1970s, when some of us were marching for women's rights, smashing down doors once bolted shut, we probably didn't expect that one of the women who'd march in behind us would be Ann Coulter, the fascist fashionista. But a world where a woman can be a star pundit—even one who thinks all liberals should be burned at the stake for treason—is arguably better than one in which all women were basically seen but not heard, no matter what their opinions.

Coulter's *I'm-outrageous-but-so-cute* act seems to have charmed more than a few male writers. She got her own cover story in *Time* magazine in 2005, and the coverline asks, "Is she serious or just having fun?"[6]

Fun, for Coulter, however, is being inflammatory 24-7. She's decreed that American Taliban John Walker Lindh ought to be executed to intimidate liberals, to show them that they can be killed. She departed her job as a columnist for the *National Review Online* after she wrote about Muslims, "We should invade their countries, kill their leaders and convert them to Christianity."[7] She's called former NBC *Today* host Katie Couric a liberal Eva Braun, referring to Hitler's mistress, dubbed beloved anchorman Walter Cronkite a left-wing blowhard, declared former Environment Secretary Christine Todd Whitman a "dimwit," and said it would be "fun" to nuke North Korea.

The *Time* piece by John Cloud was a cotton-candy valentine, basically writing off her astonishing racism and Arab-bashing as rather adorable. He said, "It would be easier to accept Coulter's reasoning if a shadow of bigotry didn't attach to many of her statements about Arabs and Muslims." Not to mention blacks, which Cloud did not. Coulter once wrote that school desegregation has led to "illiterate students knifing one another between acts of sodomy in the stairwell."[8] There's a "shadow" that's about as subtle as Sheriff Bull Connor. She also noted in a speech, "Liberals are about to become the last people to figure out that Arabs lie," and said, seriously, that airports should establish separate security lines for men and boys who look dark enough to be from the Middle East. "Swarthy men . . . We'd be searching, you know, Italians, Spanish, Jews." Cloud calls Coulter a "hardright ironist," but if this is irony, the KKK and the Aryan Nation are masters of understatement.

Her book *Slander: Liberal Lies about the American Right* shot to the top of the *New York Times* bestseller list when it was published in 2002.[9] *Slander* belongs to what has become its own literary genre: *The-left-wing-media-control-the-press*. These books are somewhat like the body-changing movies that Hollywood loves, in which men become women, women become men, grownups become kids, etc. You know the plot, you know the ending, but surprise isn't the appeal. Familiarity is. On the whole, media books sell terribly, but leftwing-plot media books do just fine, because conservatives run out and buy them. If only liberals were so loyal.

One of Coulter's heroines is conservative activist Phyllis Schlafly, who, she says, was badly treated by the media. She's probably right. Schlafly had the misfortune to be on the wrong side of history, opposing feminism just as it swept in like the tide. In the seventies, Schlafly was always cast as the anti-feminist, and her opinions on national defense, strategic global policy, and other international issues were pretty much disregarded. She was also restrained by the "ladylike" ethos of the times. She wore a country-club suit and a pasted-on smile that resembled the rigor mortis of the recently deceased. I always figured Phyllis wanted to jump at some feminist's throat and rip away, but she never could. She never got to do what Coulter does—just let it all hang out, be outrageous, call her enemies terrible names, and let the chips fall where they may. In the good old days, women didn't get to be outrageous about politics, with the possible exception of octogenarian Alice Roosevelt Longworth, Teddy's daughter.

Coutler is actually much more entertaining on the tube, where her pronouncements make grown men gasp, than she is in print. *Slander* seems to
have been written with a trowel, a hodgepodge of facts, gossip, and bile. She
can never resist the opportunity to go completely overboard after she's made
a good point, descending into caricature or hyperbole. She thinks lots of
people really hate Katie Couric and she (Coulter) "was the one to really pop
her." Do many people actually spend their days hating Katie Couric? If they
do, I am not sure I want to meet them.

Slander is choc full of footnotes, but Coulter basically just comes out
swinging a broadsword in all directions. It's hard to take her seriously when
she tosses news and gossip, serious issues and infotainment sleaze into the
same basic pot. For example, to illustrate liberal control of the media, she
serves up Bryant Gumbel interviewing *Playboy*'s Hugh Hefner about politics
during the democratic convention. Was this ideology or desperation? How
many other B-list celebrities failed to show up to fill airtime before Gumbel
stooped to the Viscount of Viagra? Another example of liberal media power
she cites is Hollywood starlets Laura Flynn Boyle and Heather Graham attacking organized religion in *Vanity Fair* and *Talk* magazines. The mainstream media, she says, gave "wild acclaim" to the opinions of these "worth-
less silicone nothings."

Lurking someplace inside *Slander* might have been an interesting treatise
on social class in the media. The press may sometimes "lie" about the right.
Christian conservatives rarely get a fair shake, but them neither do vegan
feminist antiglobalists. And there are both liberal and conservative pieties
galore—conservative pols thundering about Morality just before they dine
with their mistresses, and liberal pols praising public schools as they fill out
their own kids' applications to ritzy private schools. Coulter blasts liberals
who can't identity with the folks who mourned the death of race driver Dale
Earnhardt, but how many beltway conservatives hang around the infield at
Indy? Once upon a time, republicans represented the wealthy and democrats the working stiffs. FDR was called a traitor to his class. But now, both
parties share the largesse of the rich. Coulter gets off some zingers against
rich liberals who drive pricey SUVs and use the environment as an issue to
keep down the aspirations of the lower middle class. "Liberals want to prevent oil drilling in the mudflats of Alaska, a place they would never visit because they already have their Jacuzzis and can afford the electricity."

But Coulter's populism gets a bit confused when she voices concern
for poor blacks, but says she's bored bored BORED with talk of the civil

rights movement (which conservatives opposed) because to her it's ancient history.

Though her books are something of a mess, Coulter herself is no dummy. She says she woke up one day and decided what the world didn't need was another smart woman lawyer, and went into the pundit biz. The lust in Bill Clinton's heart—and elsewhere in his physiognomy—was tailor-made for her brand of invective, and she became a regular on *Geraldo* and a host of other shows. Coulter has decided not to take the road of her idol, Schlafly, who doggedly and seriously keeps pushing her issues, even when she's dismissed by snobbery on the left or sexism on the right. Coulter will never be a power player in the councils of the conservative movement; she's too much of a loose cannon. She happily blurts out what most people would whisper only to their buddies over a bourbon and branch water. She's decided to become an entertainer, not a bad decision. Nobody near the beltway takes her seriously of course; I've seen committed conservatives roll their eyes when her name is mentioned. You can't really envision an inflamed mob marching behind Ann in her miniskirt to lynch Muslims or tie liberals to trees and set them alight. (Though one can imagine some of the readers of her books doing just that.) She is filthy rich, from her book royalties and her lecture fees. She already has her own Barbie-type action figure, which blurts out her outrageous-isms. She is tailor-made for the modern media, which value high-decibel rant over thoughtfulness and for which no statement is too extreme, especially if it can be made with flair on television. Why should middle-aged white guys get all the shekels from tossing red meat to gun nuts, school-prayer zealots, militias out in the woods, and haters of all things swarthy? The radical right outspends the lunatic left by a country mile. At least a woman is getting a piece of the action.

WAGGING TONGUES

Coulter is the most theatrical of the conservative lady pundits, but there are many others: syndicated columnist Michele Malkin, TV and cable commentator Laura Ingraham, the *National Review*'s Kate O'Beirne, author of the 2005 book *Women Who Make the World Worse: How Their Radical Feminist Assault Is Ruining Our Schools, Families, Military, and Sports*[10] (all feminists, of course), Danielle Crittenden of the Independent Women's Forum, and author Christina Hoff Sommers, to name a few. Media consumers ought to know that these conservatives do not reflect the views of ordinary women, but of a wealthy conservative cadre whose minions have very deep pockets to attack the women's movement. It's easy for the unwary to assume that these nice, hip women they see all over the cable shows are well-meaning folks who represent lots of women. Hardly. When Christina Hoff Sommers wrote *Who Stole Feminism,* she was supported by three right-wing foundations to the tune of $160,000.[11] The Independent Women's Forum, a right-wing think tank based in Washington, was the beneficiary of a big chunk of cash from Richard Mellon Scaife, the millionaire who helped finance the impeachment campaign against Bill Clinton.[12]

A popular text with all the conservative lady pundits is that feminism harmed women. Nothing spoils a nice evening for me more than turning on the television and seeing some young woman (I am tempted to say girl) prattling on about how wonderful life was before those nasty feminists went and spoiled everything. They wax ecstatic about how wonderful life was back in the fifties when men were men and women were homemakers, and all was well with the world.

Danielle Crittenden, whose book offers *What Our Mothers Didn't Tell Us,* is the former editor of the *Quarterly* of the Independent Women's Forum, the mouthpiece of the far right, which has poured hundreds of thousands of dollars into propagandizing against day care, working mothers, sexual harassment legislation, pay equity, and just about anything that might make the life of a working woman easier.[13] Crittenden, the wife of a conservative spokesman, has a rich husband and a full-time maid to watch the kids while she grinds out her propaganda. When she wanted a job, she got hired as a columnist by her father-in-law's newspaper.

Danielle Crittenden says she knows women are miserable today because she studied 30 years of such women's magazines as *Vogue* and *Cosmo.* Scholars who do serious, accurate research about such issues as the health of working women, the effects of day care on children, etc. have no access to the kind of money the right wingers can garner. Academics don't go in for sensational soundbites, and they publish in academic presses, so they don't get ad budgets or PR blitzes, and they aren't courted by the media. But if you want real information, those are the folks to go to. You won't see them on the cable news shows, however, and only rarely on the op ed page.

If I had a time machine, I'd ship the whole pack of bright young conservative women who now get paid handsomely for writing books and commenting on TV back to the 1950s they so admire. All of a sudden, they'd be invisible. They'd be getting the coffee, doing research in a stuffy back room for some guy with a byline, or getting shuffled off to the women's page to write about weddings.

They might complain, but they'd just be told they're cute when they're mad.

BASHING BOYS?

The women on the right are the driving force behind that idea that feminists are demonizing young males, ignoring their problems to focus instead on girls. It's a phony war but the media can't resist the frame of Boys versus Girls.

Christina Hoff Sommers (*The War Against Boys: How Misguided Feminism Is Harming Our Young Men*), a fellow at the American Enterprise Institute, charges that feminists have hi-jacked the agenda of American schools, and boys are suffering as a result.[14]

The "Boy Crisis" has become a full-blown media myth, with all the elements of a good story: conflict, kids, and backlash against feminism. The media have been hyping this new "crisis" in magazine cover stories (*Newsweek* and *Business Week*), a PBS documentary, and countless newspaper articles. Boys, these reports lament, are falling behind in academic achievement, graduating from high school at lower rates than girls, occupying fewer seats in college classrooms, displaying poorer verbal skills. One Houston neurologist, Dr. Bruce Perry (quoted in *Newsweek*), called today's co-ed classes "a biologically disrespectful model of education."[15] Such arguments distort the true facts.

First of all, is there really a "boy crisis?" No. There is a "some boys' crisis."

Overall, elite boys are doing well academically. There are more males than females in Ivy League schools. And though we have been hearing that boys are disappearing from college classrooms, among whites, the numbers of males and females in college are very close, 51 percent female and 49 percent male, according to the National Education Association. In 2006, the same number of boys as girls were headed to the nation's colleges.[16] "On most measures boys—at least the middle-class white boys everyone seems concerned about—are doing just fine, taking their places in an unequal society to which they have always felt entitled," says Michael Kimmel, a SUNY sociologist who studies boys. "Many studies show that overall, girls and boys differ very little in their cognitive abilities. The gender gap in verbal abilities is closing, with boys catching up to girls."[17]

One group of studies found that, although poor and working-class boys lag behind girls in reading when they get to middle school, boys in the wealthiest schools do not fall behind, either in middle school or in high school.[18] University of Michigan education professor Valerie Lee reports that gender differences in academic performance are "small to moderate."[19]

A study released in June 2006, using federal data from the National Assessment of Educational Progress, said that widespread reports of a "boy crisis" are overstated and that boys in school are in many ways doing better than ever. The study's authors said that pessimism about non-poor, non-minority boys comes from inadequate research and poor analysis of data and that discomfort about girls' academic success seemed to be fueling an unwarranted crisis mentality.[20]

When it comes to academic achievement, race and class completely swamp gender. The Urban Institute reports that 76 percent of students who live in middle- to higher-income areas are likely to graduate from high school, while only 56 percent of students who live in lower-income areas are likely to do so.[21] Among whites in Boston public schools, for every 100 males who graduate, 104 females do. A tiny gap. But among blacks, for every 100 males who graduate, 139 females do.

Florida's graduation rates among all students show a striking picture of race and class: 81 percent of Asian students graduate, 60 percent of whites, 48 percent of Hispanics, and 46 percent of blacks.[22]

Unfortunately, however, the media "frame" on the crisis seems aimed squarely at suburban white readers. A *Newsweek* cover story featured four very middle-class-looking white boys, and when a junior at upscale Milton Academy in Massachusetts sued for sex discrimination, it was all over the front pages and the TV talk shows.[23] But one editor told a journalist pitching a story on the race and class issues in the boy crisis that the fact that poor black and Latino boys were not doing well was not news. Scare the middle class about its kids, however, and you hear the jingle of money.

Another narrative popular in the contemporary press is that girls are doing swimmingly, while boys fail. The *Business Week* cover, mentioned in the introduction, where a gigantic girl dwarfs a tiny boy, and an inside headline announces that boys are now the second sex, from kindergarten on, sets out the case.[24] Is it true? No. The story, again, changes when you look at race and class. The big picture is that about half of the US high-school population in many districts is dropping out, with girls only slightly less likely than boys to be in this group. For example, in New York City, the overall graduation rate from public schools is 43 percent. Fifty-seven percent—almost three-fifths of the entire ninth grade population—does not get a diploma within four years.

In New York, among blacks, 33 percent of males and 43 percent of females graduate. The comparable figures for Hispanics are 30 percent males and 37 percent females. So if there's a "boy crisis" it's only somewhat worse than the "girl crisis." Among blacks, 57 percent of girls don't get their sheepskins and among Latinas 63 percent of girls never make it to the podium.[25]

These figures are truly a national disgrace, and yet we seem focused on endlessly discussing gender differences in American education. Not that those differences don't warrant attention, but the elephant in the room is the dismal graduation rates overall for *both* boys and girls.

Another narrative the media adore is the "War Against Boys" in which evil feminist teachers, who just don't like boys, discriminate against them.

This is Christina Hoff Sommers's favorite hobbyhorse, and she is quoted in nearly every story on the boy crisis.

When her book came out in 2000, Hoff Sommers was everywhere: TV talk shows, cable talk shows, radio shows—an excerpt from her book even graced the cover of *Atlantic Monthly*.[26] The "War Against Boys" is an artifact of what might be called the Culture of Hype. These days, the sound bite, the coverline, the book title has to be titillating to sell. This book, with its calculated-to-scare title, fit that bill to a T.

Indeed, there are intriguing questions to ask about how to raise boys in a time of great social and economic change. Unfortunately, Hoff Sommers can't resist the impulse to indulge in a screed. While she makes some valid points about how the problems of girls have sometimes been exaggerated, the author does exactly the same thing herself with boys' problems. She generally ignores issues of race and class. She has an undue fondness for straw men, and while she bombards the reader with charts and statistics, she often makes her major points based only on a stray anecdote or two. And she's not above distorting data. For example, Hoff Sommers quotes Senator Daniel Patrick Moynihan on the dangers of a community in which young men never have any stable relationship to male authority, creating chaos.[27] She neglects to say, however, that the famous Moynihan study was on the American black underclass family. This is a major—and irresponsible—omission. She leaves the reader with the impression that Moynihan was talking about all families and all boys, when he was speaking specifically about the pathology of the underclass. For someone who chides advocates for girls for being too loosey-goosey with data, that's like living in a glass house and hurling stones.

It's hard to imagine American schools as really being the way Hoff Sommers describes them. Her favorite bete noir is feminism." She sees feminists as all-powerful, malevolently controlling everything in schools from recess to core curricula. In her worldview, classrooms are one long sensitivity session or sexual harassment seminar, with feminist teachers blaming boys for every malefaction from the Flood to the shootings at Columbine. Teachers, it seems, know few bounds in their zeal for telling little boys how rotten they are.

With no real data, she goes hunting for horror stories, and of course she finds some. There's always an overzealous teacher or principal someplace who overdoses on Political Correctness. The author cites the case of a six-year-old who was punished as a harasser for kissing a classmate as the sole basis for her statement that, "The fear of ruinous lawsuits is forcing schools to treat little boys as sexist culprits."

But, in fact, the case of the six-year-old made headlines across the nation because it was so unusual—and considered by most people to be absurd. Indeed, schools may be worrying about lawsuits, for all sorts of behavior, but six-year-olds across the nation are not being suspended for kissing. Hyperbole simply torpedoes what could have been an interesting discussion.

In another example, she cites an anecdote from a California mother who says that her son was punished for running during recess. This story is the sum total of evidence for the following statement: "Sad to say, normal male youthful exuberance is becoming unacceptable in more and more schools." But do most schools punish boys for running during recess? Highly unlikely. There is a serious discussion to be had about what school behavior is appropriate, but one doesn't find it in these pages. Another piece of hyperbole is this gem: "As the new millennium begins, the triumphant victory of our women's soccer team has come to symbolize the spirit of American girls. The defining event for boys is the shootings at Columbine High."

Sez who? If the soccer team defines girls, maybe American boys are defined by the triumphs of Tiger Woods, or by Lance Armstrong's victories—over cancer and other riders—to win the Tour de France. Do Americans regard the Columbine shooters as emblematic of their sons? Only in some paranoid fantasy.

And indeed, if feminist teachers are destroying boys, how to explain all those suburban Asian and white boys who are doing well? Did they simply manage to evade the evil feminists who dominate their schools?

The media's love affair with crisis narratives will probably not go away. Before the boy crisis there was the Girls' Self-esteem crisis. A study by the American Association of University Women in 1990 purported to show that girls faced a steep—and inevitable—decline in self-esteem at puberty.[28] The media feeding frenzy that resulted led thousands of parents to march their girls off to self-esteem seminars. But the study, it turned out, was seriously flawed, and critics pointed out that, in fact, there was no self-esteem "swan dive," and that girls and boys at puberty were remarkably similar in their levels of self-esteem.

Indeed, it will be hard enough for both sexes in a competitive world of globalization to stay afloat economically, and we should be concerned when any of our kids seem to be slipping. Boys and girls both need all the help we can give them for the uncertainties of the real world they will be facing. But pitting boys and girls against each other is dangerous. Jacqueline E. Woods, executive director of the American Association of University Women, says, "The flames of a gender war are being unnecessarily fanned, implying that educational achievement is a zero sum game and that girls' achievements have somehow come at the expense of boys. The message to women and girls is clear: You are taking more than your fair share. You're too successful. You have come too far and boys are paying the price for your accomplishments."[29] Woods argues that we have to look at both boys and girls and find ways to help them succeed. Framing educational issues as a "War Against Boys" could mean that both sexes will suffer in a needless ideological war. The media should neither exaggerate nor ignore boys' problems, nor fall prey to flawed research, no matter how sexy a story the War Against Boys seems to be.

NEW AGE DOORMATS

More surprising than the success of the female neo-cons is a remnant of the past that has resurfaced in new wrappings: Total Woman.[30]

"TW" was the seventies best seller by Marabel Morgan, who advised women that instead of getting college degrees and launching careers, they should instead study the desires of their husbands. They should be submissive and pleasing, and could thus get everything they wanted. Ms. Morgan advised wives not to nag if they craved that new washer-dryer, but to greet their husbands at the door wearing only saran wrap.

A lot of women (and undoubtedly men) thought the saran wrap was a fun idea, but had doubts about submission. However, submission reemerged in a book that became a bestseller in 2001 called *The Surrendered Wife: A Practical Guide to Finding Intimacy, Passion, and Peace with Your Man.*[31] This tome, which got plenty of media coverage, gives women the following advice:

- Relinquish control of the household finances and rely on your husband to give you what you need.
- Apologize for being disrespectful whenever you contradict, criticize, or dismiss your husband's thoughts and ideas.

- Make yourself sexually available to your husband (at least once a week).
- Defer to your husband's thinking when you have conflicting opinions.
- Most of all, practice saying the following line: "Whatever you think, dear." Say it with a smile. Try it now. Feels good, doesn't it?

No, this isn't a parody. The author, California housewife Laura Doyle, created "self-help" groups that spread across the nation and, she has a website and lecture dates, and her theories are reportedly being discussed in university classes.

"The Surrendered Wife" (along with another similar tone, Dr. Laura Schlessinger's *The Proper Care and Feeding of Husbands*[32]) is eerily reminiscent of the advice women's magazines gave to their readers in the 1950s. Here, for example, is the *Ladies Home Journal* in the mid-fifties: "The happy wife adjusts her mood to her husband's, when he feels like talking and he is uncommunicative. She conceals her disappointments. He is too tired for the movie she looks forward to, so she puts the big chair by the fire even though it spoils the effect she'd planned for the room. She follows sports and tries her luck at a new game (one her husband likes). She watches his weight, supervises his diet, provides time for him to rest."[33] Never did LHJ suggest that he take her to the movie even if he's tired or move the damn chair himself. That's *her* job.

Did all this self-abnegation lead to happy marriages 30 years ago? No. The mental health data that began to roll in during the 1970s on these traditional marriages over the preceding decades revealed massive problems of self-esteem, depression, and psychiatric symptoms for American wives. The data were so alarming that one expert, sociologist Jessie Bernard, called marriage a health hazard for women.[34]

The advice to turn all financial dealings over to a husband is especially alarming. (Even Total Woman didn't do that. She just used saran wrap to get the dough.) In case of divorce or death of a spouse, ignorance of financial matters has led to terrible economic consequences for women. And there is solid evidence that having to ask a husband for money is one of the things that eats away at a woman's self-esteem. It's infantilizing.

Laura Doyle argues that men need to be in charge and that they are miserable when they aren't. But how many men are so stupid that they would fall for the Surrendered Wife act? Also, constant obedience may get a wife something other than respect, says Christine Gailey, professor of anthropology at the University of California, Riverside.[35] Compliance does not improve marriages. "Indeed, in most cases of long-term and intense wife-battering, extreme compliance by the wife is commonplace," Gailey notes. "That is only one nasty little problem with the author's thesis."

In fact, are men happier with compliant homebodies than with women who have their own lives—and jobs? The evidence says no. Research on two-earner couples shows both partners to be satisfied with their marriages.

So why on earth would such a message gain any credence today? Why were so many feature articles devoted to this retro idea? Because it's simple and it peddles one of the oldest fairy tales—Snow White, Cinderella, et al.—the rescue fantasy. In her study of right-wing women, critic Andrea Dworkin notes that to many women, especially those with meager skills and poor marketability, the world is a scary place.[36] Male power appears omnipotent, compared to the power of women and children, and so it seems that the only way to dilute that power is to seduce it. Helplessness and compliance may entice a rescue. Unfortunately, it may also invite abuse, abandonment, and powerlessness.

Doyle, who says she is (or was) a feminist, seems to confuse bad behavior with normal, healthy assertiveness. She says, "I looked around at my friends and saw how one allowed her husband to control their finances, and another never criticized his dress sense, and I stopped nagging him [her husband] and challenging him over money and his career."

Nagging a man over his dress sense, his career, or moneymaking skills is simply insensitive, impolite, and dumb. You don't have to "surrender" to avoid doing that, you just have to have some consideration for your mate. Just as you'd expect him to be considerate of you.

In the world of backlash, however, there seems to be no happy medium. Either you are a scornful harpy who tries to dominate your husband, or you are an adoring doormat who tries to get her husband to believe he is perfect and you are a cretin. Neither tactic works, and most of us know that. Even the Southern Baptist Convention withdrew it's dictum that women should be submissive to their husbands.

If women only take away from the book the message that they should try to be nicer, and not nag, it may be a harmless read. But those who take it seriously will substitute "surrender" for a life and opinions of their own. And what's to be made of the fact that, in late 2005, Morrow reissued a 40-year-old French tome titled *The Men in Your Life: Timeless Advice and Wisdom on Managing the Opposite Sex,* which claims that "The education of young girls has always centered around the art of how to catch a husband."[37] This "art" seems to concentrate on improving their looks. If you're female and you buy such ideas, you are likely to have a rude awakening.

Not from a prince's kiss, but from turning yourself into a toad(y).

9
NEWS AS POLI-PORN

As our TV sets blared out "all Chandra, all the time," and later, as the lovely faces of Laci Peterson and Natalee Holloway, and Terri Schiavo's bright-eyed smile filled cable channels 24-7, I began to wonder, *is news becoming our new soft-core pornography?*

The 24-hour media with their omnivorous maw, and the public boredom with politics and social issues unless they are connected with the sex lives of legislators—or sex in some other form—are producing what might be called "Poli-Porn."

As viewers, we are bored to death with energy policy, legislative redistricting, most-favored-nation status, and balancing the budget. Even war in Iraq can't hold our attention for long. But give us a story about sex that can be tied in with politics, national issues, or just plain old murder with an attractive victim attached, and we sit up and take notice.

The stories that used to be simply gossip around the water cooler in the city room now lead the evening news. It's titillating to know that back in his days in the California legislature, Gary Condit, the media's favorite bad guy in the Chandra Levy murder story, was known as "Gary Condom," but is that really news? Illinois senate candidate Jack Ryan dropped out of the race in 2004 after he realized that the press was only interested in the details of his trips to sex clubs with his ex-wife, actress Jeri Ryan.

As for Gary Condit, he may have been the only person in America who gave a sigh of relief on September 11, 2001. At long last, he was off the front pages. The discovery of Chandra's remains in Rock Creek Park in Washington a year later provided a melancholy closure to a sad tale. Chandra, a young woman who was bright, personable, and from a good family, quickly became the sex object that poli-porn requires. To flourish, these tales require a picture (and video is even better) of an attractive woman to give the story legs. The image becomes, with endless replays, just another marketing tool.

LOVELY VICTIMS

The dread that we should have felt viewing the picture of a woman who had perhaps met a terrible fate should have sent a chill up our spines. But with endless exposure, the pictures of Chandra and Laci (whose husband was convicted of her murder) and Natalee, the pretty blonde teenager who vanished on a school trip to Aruba, became just more images in our pop iconography—along with Jennifer Lopez with her newest husband or Paris Hilton doing not much of anything. Even the endless replays of brain-damaged Terri Schiavo became, after a while, another media image jumbled in our brains along with others to which overexposure brings a dulling of sensations the image initially evoked.

Perhaps the most chilling such image was that of little JonBenet Ramsey doing her impersonation of the sexually provocative moves of movie stars on a home video. It was hard to remember, after a while, that this was a murdered child, not just another celebrity cover photo on *People* magazine. If Jon-Benet had not been a beautiful child (and if that video didn't exist), would her story have so enraptured the media? Probably not, but this isn't a new story. Historian Steven Mintz points out in *Huck's Raft: A History of American Childhood* that, in 1894, the story of one severely battered child, "Mary Ellen," became a huge newspaper story in the New York press, while hundreds of other such stories went unnoticed.[1] Her foster mother was imprisoned—a rare event in those days when children were assumed to be the property of their parents. As Mintz notes, "Above all, Mary Ellen was an attractive girl, and pretty young girls are particularly likely to garner public sympathy."

And while Laci Peterson's murder and the trial that followed provided hour after hour of media coverage, another story involving the death of young women received almost no coverage. Amnesty International documented at least 370 killings of young women, all of them poor or working class, through 2003, in an area near the Texas-Mexico border in the state of Chihuahua.[2] How could the saga of 200 slaughtered women be a nonstory? Because they were Latina, lower class, and sometimes involved in prostitution.

In 2006, three smart, beautiful, young Massachusetts women with promising futures were brutally murdered. As the *Boston Herald* noted,

Only the slayings of Hopkinton mother Rachel Entwistle—murdered along with her baby, Lillian Rose—and Hub college student Imette St. Guillen [killed in New York] garnered national and even worldwide media coverage for weeks on end. The equally chilling murder of former Milton High School cheerleader Dominique Samuels, whose torched body was found Sunday in Franklin Park, has been ignored by the national media. As of yesterday, [May 5] perhaps 10 newspaper articles had been written about her. Samuels, 19, was black. Entwistle was white, while St. Guillen shared both white and Hispanic heritage.[3]

The African-American woman's murder was simply not a national story. Errol Cockfield, a board member of the National Association of Black Journalists and a reporter for Newsday, said if the national media doesn't pick up the Samuels' murder, "It's proof to me that there's something wrong with newsroom managers in terms of how they think about race. It's the same old story with the national media."[4]

Often, poli-porn stories are legitimate stories that do not fade away in the usual news-cycle manner, but stay on to become mega-media events. There is no question that the disappearance of Chandra Levy and her connection to a congressman was a story. And who can blame her parents for doing all they could to keep the story alive? Without the publicity, could their daughter's case just become another missing persons file languishing in the drawers of the DC police department? The same can be said of the families of Laci Peterson, the pretty, eight-month-pregnant young woman who vanished mysteriously from her home in Modesto, California (ironically, the hometown of Chandra Levy), and the vanished teenager Natalee Holloway.

In the Levy case, the media pressure drove the police to come up with a constant flow of images to keep the news pack from snapping at their heels. We saw mounted DC police splashing through the "fords" in Washington's Rock Creek, looking for evidence. It was reported that they found a four-inch bone, and that fact was treated as a major news flash. But Rock Creek Park is home to all kinds of small wildlife, as well as the occasional deer or other quadruped that escapes from the National Zoo. Was that real police work? Or just another photo-op for a story that wouldn't quit? When poli-porn drives both news judgments and the actions of police departments and prosecutors, it distorts the agenda of both the press and law enforcement. Not to mention those of politics. In 2005, the spectacle of President Bush rushing back to Washington to endorse a bill that would have called for the reinsertion of a feeding tube into Terri Schiavo was more remarkable because thousands of such decisions are made in hospitals every day, with no media attention. If her case hadn't become poli-porn, we would never have heard of her tragic story.

Over the years, the women in poli-porn stories—especially those that involve powerful politicians and sex—have changed. Once central to such stories were what used to be called, in the days before political correctness, "floozies." What DC veteran journalist can forget the drunken plunge that Congressman Wilbur Mills took in the Tidal Basin with a stripper known as Fanne Fox? Donna Rice was described as a "party girl" when she had her fling with presidential candidate Gary Hart. The picture of the two of them aboard a boat aptly named *Monkey Business* derailed his campaign. Going way back to the sixties, the DC media were all agog over Carole Tyler, a beautiful young woman who was the administrative assistant to Bobby Baker, a top aide to President Lyndon Johnson. That story of high living in high places lasted a few days in the media then. Today, it would have been full blown poli-porn, featuring famous men, a woman with "bee-stung lips" (as one reporter described them), and lots of all-night parties in hotels in Ocean City, Maryland.

In those days, females known as "women with a past" were central to scandals. They have been replaced, it seems, with women of a higher social class in the most over-hyped news stories. Once upon a time, women of certain breeding and income level might have been protected if they had an indiscretion with a powerful man. I've known a number of women who had such liaisons, and few of them worried about ending up on the pages of the *National Enquirer.* Today, the bottom-feeding tabs have lots of money and they throw it around. Monica Lewinsky thought she was confiding romantic secrets to a friend, but she ended up, for a time, as the most famous woman in the world. Monica made a much better subject for poli-porn than Paula Jones—widely disparaged as trailer trash—because Monica was better educated, of a higher social class, and more sympathetic.

Anne Marie Smith, the flight attendant who was having a discreet affair with Gary Condit, also came across as bright and well-spoken. She was much better fodder for the talk shows than a less articulate woman would have been. Poli-porn today is more saleable with a touch of class; maybe because we all like to think we've moved upscale. (Most of the trash-talk TV shows featuring the poorest and most dysfunctional among us faded fast.) Ms. Smith was desperate to stay out of the spotlight, but her roommates sold her story and picture to the tabloids and made a pile of money.

Beautiful Dreamer?

What if Terri Schiavo had been a) African American, b) Latina, c) Overweight and unattractive, or d) white and living in a trailer park? Would she have become the symbol of such gut-wrenching national issues as the right to die, the rights of the disabled, the role of the state in family matters, and the rights of husbands versus those of parents? Most likely not.

Two images propelled the story into national prominence. The first was of a beautiful 26-year-old woman smiling at the camera, the other the video of an older Terri, bedridden, but appearing to smile and respond to an off-screen voice. Who could not be moved by the sight of vibrant life so tragically devastated, and by the anguish of her parents, who wanted their daughter alive, no matter how bleak that life seemed to be?

Almost all the still photographs of Terri Schiavo that the media featured were of her looking beautiful and sexy—smiling at the camera, cuddling with her husband, or stretched out on a beach chair in a swimsuit looking slim and fit. Rarely did I see the video of the high-school Terri, who was quite overweight and hardly a sex symbol. Such pictures were obviously available to the media, but few outlets, it seems, chose to run them. An unattractive victim doesn't get ratings. Ironically, Terri's struggle to be thin was what appears to have led to the heart attack that caused her severe brain damage.

An eating disorder was believed to have led to the attack, and Michael Schiavo collected in the neighborhood of a million dollars in a malpractice suit against her doctors for not diagnosing her properly.

We may never know what Terri Schiavo's real wishes were. The only silver lining to the story of her death may have been the overwhelming public unhappiness with politicians trying to make hay from private tragedy. Polls clearly signaled the public's dismay with the involvement of President Bush, his bother Jeb (the governor of Florida), House Majority Leader Tom DeLay, and the US Congress as a whole stepping in where angels fear to tread. Many of us were horrified at the idea of our state representative, our congressman, or even our president looking over the shoulders of our family members if and when they ever have to decide whether *we* should be kept alive by artificial means.

Perhaps the next time the media focus on an attractive victim in a vegetative state, politicians will keep their distance. Not so the media, because such stories engender ratings. This was a TV-driven story, and while many news shows tried conscientiously to explain, for example, the difference between the cerebral cortex and the brain stem, and to give a realistic picture of Terri's true condition, others pandered to those with a political agenda. As I was surfing the cable stations one night, I came upon Fox's Sean Hannity suggesting that if Terri could only get some good therapy, she indeed might be able to sit up, eat, speak, and resume something resembling a normal life. But no one with any medical credentials—not even the physicians who believed Terri retained some brain function and that her feeding tube should *not* be removed—ever made such a claim. After 15 years in a vegetative state, with her cerebral cortex almost completely destroyed, only a miracle akin to the raising of Lazarus could have accomplished such a feat.

The Runaway Bride

Only a short time after the Schiavo story faded from view, the media had another attractive, affluent "victim," Jennifer Wilbanks, who became known to the entire nation in the spring of 2005 as "The Runaway Bride." Her disappearance was a legitimate media story, as thousands searched the area around Gainesville, Georgia, after she vanished shortly before her lavish, 500-guest wedding. Friends, her fiancé, and the police feared she had been the victim of foul play. But again, ask the questions I asked earlier about Terri Schiavo—if she had been black, Latina, unattractive, overweight, etc, would it have been anything other than a short-lived local story? After all, thousands of women disappear every year, especially poor and minority women, and they rarely make the news pages.

But once it was determined that Jennifer was alive and only suffering from cold feet—perhaps brought on by depression or anxiety—end of story, right? Wrong. The poor woman became a media obsession, with her very own *People* magazine cover and the details of her life spread across the national media.[5] *People* used eleven reporters in Gainesville, Albuquerque, Orlando, and New York to write and report the story. We learned about Wilbanks's wedding plans, her relationship to her fiancé, what presents the invitees had bought, and if they were going to ask for their money back. The wide-eyed, smiling, still photograph of Wilbanks seemed omnipresent. CNN's Dr. Sanjay Gupta even dissected a close-up of Jennifer's eyes, pointing out the degree of white visible above the pupil, suggesting she might have Graves' disease. *People* magazine quoted a friend: "The bridesmaids are angry. They had been going to countless parties and bought expensive dresses. She was their best friend and they feel duped." This is news? At the same time, the insurgency in Iraq was widening, the nation was embroiled in a battle over Social Security, and Iran and Korea seemed on the verge of going nuclear.

Poli-porn, it seems, has become an established part of our political life, but does it do any real harm—other than to those unlucky enough to be caught up in its snares?

Yes, it does. Poli-porn trivializes terrible events, confusing tragic reality with entertainment. It reduces our dread and awe of life's terrible moments to the same bored reaction we have to most made-for-TV movies. There, the violence is predictable and, by now, routine. Actresses with familiar faces and high "Q" ratings (that is, they are well known to audiences) suffer awful fates between commercials for hair color and allergy medicines. We know perfectly well that when we click off the TV, those women will go back to their homes in the Hollywood Hills and live quite comfortably until they are called upon once again to suffer onscreen.

In addition to conflating tragedy and entertainment, poli-porn also turns our news media into trivia and even further heightens the cynicism of a public disgusted by the political process. None of this is good for our democracy—or our souls.

THE OLD GREY MARE

The news media's obsession with beautiful young women also sends a powerful message about growing old. The late philosopher Susan Sontag called it "The Double Standard of Aging."[6]

In television, of course, the law is obvious. Gaze at your typical anchor pair—they look some guy and his second wife. Or in some cases, grandfather and granddaughter. The face-lift has become more important for female newscasters than the journalism degree. Brokaw, Rather, and Jennings were at the helm for years and could be lined and rumpled, but can you even imagine a female anchor who shows the same degree of aging? In fact, another category should be added to the endangered species list. Underneath the Spotted Owl and the Bald Eagle, affix the words "Grey Anchorwoman."

Troll around your 100-plus channels and you will find plenty of silver locks, from full-head manes to salt-and-pepper sprinkles, but they will be on the men, not the women. On them, you'll find a multitude of blondes, a bevy of brunettes, and a smattering of redheads—but hardly a grey hair in the lot. In a society already youth-obsessed, television news may be helping to foster the idea that aging in women is a process filled with dread and fear.

But even in print, the growing power of infotainment means that, increasingly, the women who appear in news columns come more and more from film, music, and other areas of entertainment, and are often very young. Women as a group have fared very badly under the double standard. The saga of Katherine Harris, a central figure in the Florida election drama of 2000, is a case in point.

Not since a pale Richard Nixon locked horns with a tanned John F.

Kennedy in the first televised presidential debate had makeup been a major subject of political dialogue in the United States. But journalists, talk show hosts, and comedians had a field day with the powder and mascara used by Florida Secretary of State (now Congresswoman) Katherine Harris. She burst onto the national scene trying to certify George W. Bush as the winner of the state's electoral votes, undoubtedly not expecting her cosmetics to get almost as much ink as "pregnant chads."

Harris—whether you see her as a heroine or a diehard partisan—became the inheritor of a growing trend in American politics. The men can look like unmade beds and that fact goes unmentioned, while the bodies, hair, and makeup of women get intense scrutiny.

The focus on Harris was unrelenting, and largely unflattering. A profile in the *Washington Post* noted that Harris's lipstick was of "the creamy sort that smears all over a coffee cup and leaves smudges on shirt collars," that she "applied her makeup with a trowel," and it compared the texture of her skin to a plastered wall.[7]

A democratic operative labeled her Cruella deVil, the villainess of *101 Dalmatians,* and the term got repeated everywhere. The *Boston Globe* said maybe she was planning to unwind at a drag bar,[8] and the *Boston Herald* called her a painted lady.[9] Jay Leno called the election "tighter than Katherine Harris's face."

But there was almost no media comment on the physiognomy of political men involved in the drama. The spokesmen for the two campaigns, James Baker and Warren Christopher, were men of a certain age who indeed looked their ages. There was no comment about the fact that they were hardly young. The physique of republican VP Dick Cheney only became the subject of news articles when a mild heart attack led to the question of his weight gain. Had that not happened, his girth would have been most unnewsworthy.

The double standard that Harris encountered was almost an exact replay of one of the biggest political stories of the past decade, the Clinton impeachment saga. Once again there were major female and male players—but the only ones whose faces and bodies were routinely scrutinized were the women: Monica Lewinsky, Linda Tripp, Paula Jones, and Hillary Clinton. Three out of four of these women actually felt compelled to alter their faces or bodies after the searing light of the media spotlight fell on them. Paula Jones, who accused President Clinton of sexual harassment, got a nose job. Monica Lewinsky, after endless media stories about her weight, joined a commercial weight-loss program and became its spokesperson for a time. Linda Tripp, who "ratted" on Lewinsky, endured constant comments on her weight, hair, and dress—to the point where she reportedly got a total makeover, including liposuction, to project a better image.

On the night the president made his "mea culpa" speech, Arsenio Hall said in a TV interview that Monica was fat and Paula was ugly, sentiments often repeated.

Jay Leno, no sylph himself, referred to Linda Tripp as an elephant. And when Hillary Clinton was photographed in a bathing suit in the middle of the impeachment drama, public comments about her thighs abounded.

In contrast, few comments were made in public about the imperfections of the bodies of the men involved. While there were occasional comments about Bill Clinton's thighs after he was photographed in jogging shorts, he was most often referred to as a handsome man. And compare Linda Tripp with special prosecutor Ken Starr. Like Tripp, he was middle-aged, very average in appearance, and hardly a snappy dresser. Neither of these two people would have stood out in a crowd of bureaucrats on Washington's F Street. But there was almost no comment at all about Ken Starrs's abs, or lack of them, while Linda Tripp was a moving target.

One of the major Whitewater figures, Webster Hubbell, was far more overweight than Linda Tripp, but his size was rarely remarked upon, while hers was constantly mentioned.

And then there was Monica Lewinsky, a young woman built along the lines of fifties' sex goddess Jane Russell. But today, Jane—and her co-star Marilyn Monroe—would be marched off to a fat farm. Actress-model Elizabeth Hurley, talking about Marilyn Monroe, told *Allure* magazine, "I would kill myself if I was that fat."[10] Like most women endowed with ample chests, Monroe and Russell also had hips. The ideal beauty today is an artificial creature: a woman with the legs, hips, and stomach of an eleven-year-old boy, but with outsized breasts created by surgery. The average model in 1986 weighed only 8 percent less than average women; today, she weighs 23 percent less.[11] Monica Lewinsky may have been a pudgy teenager, but today she's fat only by a standard that renders real female bodies unacceptable.

In fact, today fashion editors now use technology to stretch photos of supermodels—who, one would think, are skinny enough to begin with. One magazine took several inches off the waist and hips of that noted chubbete Demi Moore for a cover photo. Fifty years ago, the hip size of the average mannequin was 37 inches—the same as the average woman. Now it's 31 inches. In Hollywood casting sessions today, a size six is considered on the edge of plumpness. The ideal is size zero. The Invisible Shrinking Woman has become a staple of the media. The infotainment media present an exaggerated view of hyper-thin women. This is done not only in the ads in which the news is embedded but, because of the rise of infotainment, in the news columns themselves. I was surprised when a student of mine—who seemed to me to be a very attractive, normal-sized twenty-year-old—told me she was a plus-size model. She said she had been on shoots with prepubescent thirteen-year-olds—who as yet had no hips or breasts—made up to look like adults. (And if breasts were desired, they could be added by digital technology.) The child models got more money than my student, who was the *real* woman. Model Carrie Otis, who graced a *Sports Illustrated* swimsuit spread in her thirties, confessed she had to starve herself and take cocaine to stay a size 4 to be accepted. She later ditched the drugs, started eating normally, and became a very beautiful size 12—but of course had to become a plus-size model. You only have to look at some of the women on primetime television, at Paris Hilton, and a few of the Desperate Housewives, to see the hyper-thinness that is now being presented as ideal. Some modeling agents reportedly look on hospital wards for young anorexics to be the next supermodels. On magazine covers, technology shaves inches off already perfect bodies, changing forever our idea of what the ideal should be.

Men are allowed considerable latitude in appearance and natural aging, while women are judged by much harsher standards. As Susan Sontag pointed out, there are two standards of appearance by which men are judged—the boy and the man. The boy has a slim waist, smooth skin, and thick hair. But the man can be considered handsome with a thickening waist, wrinkles, and a hairline that's barely there. Sean Connery, in his sixties, was dubbed the sexiest man alive by *People* magazine. Harrison Ford, nearing sixty, still plays sexy action-adventure heroes.

For women there's only one standard: the girl. Whether she's 19 or 49, the woman is judged by the *girl* standard. Why are so many female commentators young and blonde, while almost no male pundits look like boys? Why are men perfectly acceptable candidates to opine despite double chins, balding pates, and thick waists or glasses, while women have to look like they've barely made it out of graduate school?

When Greta Van Susteren moved from CNN to Fox, she reemerged with a face-lift and a brand new hairdo. Critic Robin Gerbner notes that, "before her surgery, Van Susteren had been an increasingly visible beacon, projecting the hope that women had made progress. You believed that she had made it in television because she was so darn smart, clearly the best legal analyst on the air." However, Gerbner says, for a woman, "Being smart, smarter, smartest isn't enough."[12] Katie Couric shed her old girl-next-door image at *Today* for a glamorous persona, very short skirts, and, some say, a new nose. When she won the anchor chair at CBS, the network released a photo of Couric that had been "Photoshopped" to make her look thinner. Even a lovely, fit woman like Katie wasn't good enough for the media in her natural state.

A journalist I know told me that, when she was appearing on a television network panel show, one of the producers said that former UN ambassador Jeanne Kirkpatrick was dropped from consideration because she looked too old. Would Henry Kissinger have gotten the same treatment?

So the double standard of aging has real consequences. Its main effect is to silence women. How many men would put themselves forward in the public arena knowing that the texture of their skin and their girth would be constantly examined? Women who step forward must pay the price of critical scrutiny, while men are nearly always exempt.

The double standard strikes women at the exact point in their lives when they can begin to exert real power—middle age or beyond. Aside from the occasional supermodel or actress, women in their twenties rarely have much power in the public arena, just as most young men do not. But as men age, they inherit the cloak of invisibility—or at least acceptability. They can graduate from boy to man with some measure of grace. But women are only allowed to go from girl to trying-to-stay-a-girl. A columnist in the *Boston Herald* wrote of Katherine Harris. "There seemed to be something humiliating, sad, desperate and embarrassing about Harris yesterday, a woman of a certain age trying too hard to hang on."[13] At the time, Katherine Harris was 43, not exactly a crone.

Women are mocked in the media for aging; they are not acceptable unless they have been face-lifted or lipo-suctioned, had "eye-opener" surgery or dyed their hair. This is a chilling mechanism for keeping women unseen and unheard at the very time they might exert power.

10
BRAINPOWER

Once again, women's brains are being used against them.

The idea that female brains don't quite measure up is like one of the heads on that ancient beast, the chimera. Lop off one head and another magically appears to take its place.

It used to be said that women's brains were so small they could only reach the intellectual level of children or animals. Now it's being alleged that women's brains make them ideally suited to nice, comfy things like relationships, but not to hard stuff like math and science. Or writing op ed pieces for newspapers.

Alleged brain differences were at issue in the fractious squabble over why there aren't more women writers on the op ed pages of America's newspapers (see chapter 6). A *Washington Post* article in March of 2005 ventured the idea that women's brains made them too cautious to express strong opinions.[1] "Women, being tuned in to the more cautious (and more creative) right brain," said the *Post* story, "are more reluctant to do something unless they're sure they're going to get it right."

Too often, with brain research, sweeping assertions are made on what one researcher calls "a thimbleful of evidence." New "discoveries" about the human brain appear and are debunked faster than hemlines go up and down. Here's an alternate theory about why women don't write as many opinion pieces as men. New research finds that women in areas that are generally thought to be male are seen as either competent and unlikable, or incompetent and likeable. In other words, a woman with strong opinions on the op ed page is far more likely to be disliked than a man—and perhaps less likely to get the nod from male editors. Perhaps most important, it's harder for women to get on the rolodexes of op ed editors than it generally is for men. And, of course, there's the one-woman-speaks-for-all syndrome. Often, you see three white guys weighing in on the same subject on the same page in the same week, but once Ellen Goodman or Maureen Dowd writes on a subject, the door is closed. The fracas over op eds illustrates the ways in which generalizations about women's brains are being used to avoid the whole subject of discrimination. Switching the topic to brain structures or hormones usually means taking the focus away the real reasons that women are often absent from the top levels in many fields.

A book that was widely reviewed in the media, *The Wonder of Girls* by Michael Gurian, presents the same notion that female brains aren't really meant for the hard stuff.[2] Gurian believes that nature intends girls primarily for having and nurturing children, and that if they put too much emphasis on achievement and careers they will suffer lifelong misery.

Gurian told an education conference in Canada that no more than 20 percent of girls can aspire to be engineers or architects, and that women lack natural technical ability. He proffers a theory he calls "bridge brains" to document this notion. He says that only girls with brains that work like boys' brains can understand spatial concepts such as math and sciences. He claims that the structure of most girls' minds makes it too hard for them to grasp subjects like calculus and physics.

Does this idea sound loony? To a number of experts it does. One staffer at the Toronto School Board called Gurian's ideas "Voodoo science." Therezia Zoric told the *Toronto Star,* "It's bad research. He just hasn't met a reasonable standard of common-sense truth."[3]

But a news report on the Canadian conference said that teachers were "lining up" to buy his books. The *Chicago Tribune* says his books have won "universal praise," in an article that often cites his theories as if they were fact.[4] The *Tribune* did not note that Gurian is a family therapist with no training in neuroscience. (He claims that new technologies allow us to locate the human soul, which is made of light.) The *Tribune* writer also repeats at face value Gurian's statement that girls' brain structures account for a major difference in self-esteem between girls and boys. At the time this story was written (2002), however, the idea that girls inevitably suffer a loss of self-esteem in preadolescence had come under heavy fire. Critics had called a study by the American Association of University Women that had made the claim seriously flawed, and a subsequent meta-analysis of many studies found no difference in self-esteem between boys and girls.[5] The reporter obviously didn't know this.

As journalism gets more competitive, as newspapers and broadcast outlets find it harder to scrape up the funds to hire reporters with expertise in the biosciences, more and more questionable stories get printed. If books with flawed science sell well, their authors are too often seen by reporters as "experts" and their statements taken seriously even when they have scant credentials. Even the usually reliable *Library Journal* recommended Gurian's book on girls "because of Gurian's name and because it bridges the areas of self-help and biology."[6]

The *Washington Post* quotes Gurian in 2005 as saying that we have to teach boys to read differently from girls because of innate gender differences.[7] But the issue is much more complicated. Boys mature later than girls and overall may not do as well in early grades in reading, but they often catch up. On the SATs, boys outperform girls. This is a very complex topic, warns Claremont-McKenna's Diane Halpern, who did a definitive review of cognitive sex differences, and she warns against the easy fixes the media love. "One thing we clearly know is that there is no single or simple answer about cognitive sex differences . . . At one moment the data seem to favor one conclusion, yet on reflection, or the accumulation of contradictory data, each theory seems inadequate, subject to alternative explanations. Or completely wrong."[8] The thing to keep in mind, she cautions, is that males and females are vastly more alike than different when it comes to such abilities.

A DISMAL SCIENCE

Michael Gurian is only the latest addition to a dismal list of people who try to use brain "science" to make sweeping statements about human nature. Most of the time, such statements turn out to be dead wrong. Harvard scientist Stephen Jay Gould has described how nineteenth-century scientists took skulls, packed them full of lead, and weighed and measured them.[9] They concluded that blacks and women had tiny, immature brains and were thus not capable of the higher intellectual functions achieved by white men. As one Parisian scientist decreed in 1879, "There are a large number of women whose brains are closer in size to those of gorillas, than to most developed male brains. This inferiority is so obvious that no one can contest it for a moment, only its degree is worth discussing."

Today, nobody argues that women have tiny brains that make them unfit to go to college. Women fill more college seats then men. But they *are* being told that their brains are suited primarily to motherhood and relationships, and that their whole lives should be geared toward this end. Misery is the price to be paid if they deviate from this path. Michael Gurian presents some 30 studies that he says "prove" his thesis that women's brains are utterly different from men's. But few scientists would agree with such ideas as "bridge brains." Neuropsychologist Doreen Kimura, a researcher based in British Columbia, told the *Christian Science Monitor* that you can indeed find structural differences in the brains of men and women, but "in the larger comparative context, the similarities between human males and females far outweigh the differences."[10]

Anyone familiar with the debates over brain science in the past few years may feel as if he or she has been watching a ping-pong match. Various theories about brain function were announced with fanfare and then were rapidly abandoned. The left-brain-right-brain debate captured a lot of media attention. Which side of the brain was most important, and which side did men and women use?

Of course, whichever side was in favor at the moment, men were said to be better at using it, as psychologist Carol Tavris pointed out in her groundbreaking book, *The Mismeasure of Woman*.[11]

Originally, the left hemisphere was considered the repository of intellect and reason. The right hemisphere was the sick, bad, crazy side. The side of passion, instincts, criminality and irrationality. Guess which sex was thought to have left-brain intellectual superiority? (Answer: males.) In the 60's and 70's, however, the right brain was resuscitated and brought back into the limelight. Scientists began to suspect it was the source of genius and inspiration, creativity and imagination, mysticism and mathematical brilliance. Guess which sex was now thought to have right brain specialization. (Answer: Males.)

Even when women are decreed to be better at some intellectual function, they lose out for some other reason. For example, women's alleged superior motor coordination might make a number of them well suited to neurosurgery. But in a book called *Brain Sex*, doctors Anne Moir and David Jessel write, "It may be true that women would make better neurosurgeons than men." But they caution, "To reach the heights of a profession of this nature requires a single-minded desire to be top, and for every woman who wants to be a top neurosurgeon there will forever be ten men who want to be top neurosurgeons." Women just don't have the drive and ambition for it, they claim.[12]

In fact, simplistic ideas about how the brains of men and women propel each sex toward a narrow range of behavior is indeed voodoo science. The truth is that variation is the rule where the sexes are concerned. Men and women differ among themselves more than they differ from the opposite sex.

The science of the brain is a field where we are early pioneers, and we really don't know that much about this amazingly complex organ. The more we learn, the more we understand that we should not make sweeping generalizations. Girls are not so uniquely wired for nurture that they will be miserable if they delay marriage and children to order to pursue careers and education—or if they don't marry. Single women can have happy, fulfilling lives. Nurture is critical to the lives of both men and women, but it is hardly the only ingredient of good mental health. In fact, if we give girls the message that they must be so preoccupied with nurture that they should scale back their dreams and ambitions, we may be setting them up for future problems. Full-time homemakers, for example, report much higher levels of depression and anxiety than do working women. All their nurturing does not always offer protection from psychological problems. Women are not one-sided creatures who only need to love and relate to be happy. They also need to learn, to accomplish, and to achieve. Just as men aren't one-dimensional creatures who don't need relationships and can be satisfied only with achievement.

What happens, one wonders, to the teachers who buy Michael Gurian's book? Will they pay less heed to the academic talents of their female students than to those of the boys, having bought the notion that girls are suited mainly to nurture? And will parents discourage their daughters from high achievement, fearing that the price will be an unhappy life?

The same theme echoes through a more academic look at the subject, in a book that was featured in a major 2005 op ed in the New York Times and on the cover of Newsweek. Simon Baron-Cohen of Cambridge University announces in The Essential Difference that there are two kinds of brains.[13] He believes the male brain is the "systematizing brain," while the female brain is the "empathizing" brain. The advantages of the male ("systematizing") brain, he says, include a mastery of these skills: hunting and tracking, trading, achieving and maintaining power, gaining expertise, tolerating solitude, using aggression, and taking on leadership roles. The advantages of the female ("empathizing") brain include making friends, mothering, gossip, and "reading" your partner.

Interesting how all the leadership roles in society require the male brain, while the female brain lends itself to the domestic arena. Baron-Cohen says male and female brains are perfectly suited for certain "specialist" niches— one adapted to predicting and controlling events and the other to survival and integration in the social world. But in fact, he's describing power, not gender. The powerful control events; the powerless try to survive under the rules the powerful have created.

Not only are empathizing women expected to pick up on what others are *obviously* feeling, but according to Baron-Cohen, women are hardwired to respond to "any emotion or state of mind, not just the more obvious ones, such as pain."[14] Any other person's emotion—whether he or she is close to you or distant—triggers empathy in the "natural" woman. Describing this mechanism, he says, "Imagine that you not only see Jane's pain but you also automatically feel concern, wince, and feel a desire to run across and help alleviate her pain." Would any woman so fully occupied with caring for everybody around her have the ability to lead others? Hardly. She'd barely have the time or the energy to get dressed in the morning. She'd also be a prime candidate for depression and burnout. And where are men in this picture? Stuck in the old male stereotype—detached, rational, unfeeling, unconcerned with others. In Baron-Cohen's worldview, all of the involved fathers we see around us should not exist—or should be very rare—and humane, caring, male managers would be in short supply. Men who read that they are not designed for empathy may simply give up. If their brain structure preordains them to detachment, why in the world would they try to develop the caring skills for which they are totally unsuited?

Baron-Cohen's book illustrates a disturbingly common trend in the media today. To gain commercial success, ideas often have to be hyped well beyond their legitimate scope. Baron-Cohen is an expert in autism, and his ideas about this disease and its possible link to the brain structures of males are intriguing. (Even so, in a letter to *Newsweek,* a professor of clinical neuroscience at Columbia University warned: "To give the impression that [autism] 'may be just an extreme version of the normal male intelligence' . . . may be perilously misleading."[15] He notes that such ideas are controversial in the field and "[t]he critical reader would do well to gain a comprehensive perspective in mainstream thought concerning autism from additional sources.") But the title of Baron-Cohen's book does not even mention autism; rather, the book is presented as a sweeping overview of the brains of men and women. As such, it is extremely unsophisticated when he gets beyond his area of expertise. Baron-Cohen's ideas about empathy are a distressing example of generalization based on almost no credible data. These are the jobs that Baron-Cohen suggests for women: "Counselors, primary school teachers, nurses, carers, therapists, social workers, mediators, group facilitators or personnel staff." Note that most of these are low-paid female ghetto jobs with little power.

In his *Times* op ed, Baron-Cohen cites, as evidence of great brain difference between the sexes, one study of day-old babies in which the boys looked at mobiles longer and the girls looked at faces longer.[16] This finding was said to validate the notion that male brains are suited for spatial abilities, math, and understanding systems, while female brains are naturally geared to interpersonal relationships. The media has hyped this study incredibly, here and abroad. A BBC documentary, *Secrets of the Sexes,* aired in July of 2005 and presented Baron-Cohen's ideas as fact. The *Guardian* reported, "We may think we are individuals, governed by our own drives and ambitions, but according to the biology and neurology presented [on the BBC show], we are just prisoners of our gender."[17]

Baron-Cohen's lone study, featured by the BBC and the *Times,* also led to headlines such as; "How Science Has Helped Us Discover that Boys Will Be Boys and Girls Will Be Girls" (*Ottawa Citizen*)[18]; "Mars, Venus Still Gender Benders" (*The Australian*)[19]; and "The Gender's Not for Bending; Men and Women Have Different Kinds of Biological Brains After All (*London Telegraph*).[20]

Amazingly, this same study was also reported in an *Economist* article and a *Parents Magazine* story, in which it was cited as evidence of boys' superior spatial skills.[21] "Born to Build," the magazine said of boys. (Girls' "superior" verbal skills were noted, but in a muted way. No headline announced "Born to Write.") Articles in *Maclean's,* the *Boston Globe,* the *Washington Post,* the *Wall Street Journal,* and a number of other media outlets have also reported on the day-old babies. Almost never do media stories examine whether the study is valid, and Dr. Rosalind Barnett and I found this one to be especially flawed.

In fact, the study, done in Baron-Cohen's laboratory in 2000, is almost meaningless. One of its most articulate critics is psychologist Elizabeth Spelke, co-director of the Mind, Brain and Behavior Interfaculty Initiative at Harvard, an expert on infant cognition.[22] She writes, "Baron-Cohen is not the first to claim that men are rational and women are emotional, but the experiment . . . seems to give the claim its first clear support." She then goes on to utterly demolish that support:

- The study has never been replicated nor has it appeared in a peer-reviewed journal. When a study can't be replicated, red flags should go up.
- The experiment lacked critical controls against experimenter bias and was not well designed. Female and male infants were propped up in a parent's lap and shown, side by side, an active person or an inanimate object. Since newborns can't hold their head up independently, their visual preferences might have been determined by the way their parents held them.
- There's a long literature that contradicts the study and provides

evidence that male and female infants tend to respond equally to people and objects. Better-designed studies show no male superiority in spatial and mathematics abilities at an early age. Some studies, in fact, show that female babies understand, before boy babies do, that the distance an object travels depends on the force with which it is hit.[23] Female infants pass this milestone at 5.5 months and males at 6.5 months. Where are the headlines that announce "Females Have Advantage in Mechanical Reasoning"? And most studies find no gender difference. These results come from studies that are rigorous in design and guard against experimenter bias.

Spelke writes, point blank, "These findings do not support Baron-Cohen's thesis that male infants are predisposed to learn more rapidly about the workings of the world. Male infants have no systematic advantage over female infants."

By and large, the media ignored this solid scientific evidence in favor of reporting the wrong-headed notion that boys are born to build and to do math and are hardwired for systemizing, while girls are not. The upshot of all this coverage is that when reporters or columnists sit down to write about boys and girls, they will pull up a batch of articles that are supposed to be reporting on the "science" of gender differences. The writers may well assume that there is a scientific consensus that, from infanthood on, males have an innate edge in spatial abilities and mathematical reasoning. All the flawed stories that have achieved immortality in the world of the internet will tell them this is indeed the case.

But the news media continue to be enthralled with brain research, no matter how preliminary. A good example is the headlines generated by a study done by Stanford University researchers who took brain scans of men and women looking at photographs. Three weeks later, they said, the women remembered photographs that had an emotional connotation better than the men did. Shortly afterward, a London newspaper claimed that women were more emotional and programmed to remember things men did not.[24] (One of the "emotional" pictures was of dirty toilets, and maybe the women remembered that because they figured they'd have to clean it, while the men did not.) CNN, the Associated Press, and many other outlets picked up the story of how females' brains are designed to deal with emotion. But first of all, a study of 24 people tells us very little. Second, men are not born with emotional numbness—though some can indeed manage to acquire it. Harvard professor William Pollack, author of *Real Boys, Rescuing Our Sons from the Myths of Boyhood,* points out that research tells us that boy babies are in fact more expressive and vocal with people than girl babies.[25] A review of all the systematically collected research shows that women are not more empathetic than men and men are not less able to relate to others than females.[26]

But the stories about women and their natural emotions serve a backlash agenda. If women are all about feelings, then of course they are *not* all about leadership, rationality or achievement. Sensationalizing by the media of brain research can be dismissed by scientists as trivial and inaccurate, but it can have real-life—and unhappy—consequences, especially for girls. Making sweeping statements about male and female brains, writes Carol Tavris, "is silly science and it serves us badly."

Indeed. For more silly science, read on.

MATH WARS

In January of 2005, the president of Harvard vaulted into the headlines, and the result was Math Wars II: The Return of the Stereotype.

Lawrence Summers caused an international uproar over his remarks at an academic forum, where he suggested that women failed to achieve high-level jobs in substantial numbers in science and math *not* because of discrimination, but because of inborn sex differences. Both male and female academics complained loudly that Summers was shooting from the hip and drawing very simplistic (if not dead wrong) conclusions from complicated research. Summers later made a public apology and said he had the scientific facts wrong.

But how many people will remember only the initial headlines, not the critique and the apology? How many school advisors will keep on telling female students not to bother taking tough math courses, and how many parents will steer their daughters toward careers in other fields?

Those who follow the issue of gender and math know that the best research says that there are few differences between males and females. The problem is that the best research is not always what gets reported. Most researchers examining gender differences in math rely on reports of group "mean" differences: They test groups of boys and girls and may find that, on average, boys outperform girls. (Say, for example, that the average score for boys is 104, and for girls 97.) Analyses may find that this difference is statistically significant, meaning that it is unlikely to be due to chance. The result? Headlines blaring "Boys Outscore Girls in Math," suggesting that the gulf in scores is wide and important. But the reporter who wrote the story is probably not sophisticated about the mysteries of statistics, and hasn't asked the key question: What does that difference mean? Is it large, or so small as to be basically meaningless, though statistically significant? Remember, the key issue is not the size of the difference in the average scores of the boys and girls. What counts is how that difference relates to the *range* of scores in each group.

This is very much the case with the SATs, in which boys often outscore girls. First, these tests were designed *only* to predict math scores in the first year of college, not to indicate who would—and who would not—succeed in math and science careers. And they don't do a very good job at the former. If the SAT were an accurate predictor of how well students would actually do in college, then women should fare much worse than men. In fact, freshmen women perform at least as well as men and often better. The SAT under-predicts how well girls will do and overpredicts how well boys will do.[27] (Some people believe that the SAT resembles a computer game that puts a premium on strategic guesswork. When girls get coaching on how to take the test, their scores improve.) Since numbers can lie, or at least mislead, to get the real story we need to look at studies that take a more sophisticated approach. These are usually major reviews, large-scale studies with representative samples, and meta-analyses, which combine results from many studies.

When you look at such sophisticated research, as Dr. Rosalind Barnett and I did in our 2004 book *Same Difference,* what do you find? The evidence is convincing that women are not innately inferior to men in math:

- Psychologist Janet Hyde of the University of Wisconsin, in a meta-analysis (a combination of many studies) of the math scores of four million students, found few differences. Boys outperformed girls in 51 percent of the studies, girls outperformed boys in 43 percent, and there was no gender difference in 5 percent of the studies. Sex differences were tiny.[28] (See fig. 2.)
- Psychologist Diane Halpern of Claremont McKenna College, in a definitive overview of math and cognitive abilities that are supposed to show substantial sex differences, found such differences to be trivial. Overall, she says, while there are slight differences, boys and girls are far more alike than different.[29]
- Some argue that male hormones give men an inborn advantage at math. Since these hormones kick in at puberty, we should see a striking difference in boys' and girls' math scores at this time. Researchers Erin Leahey and Guang Guo at the University of North Carolina, Chapel Hill, followed 20,000 four-to-eighteen-year-olds to

FIG. 2 GENDER DIFFERENCES IN MATHEMATICS PERFORMANCE

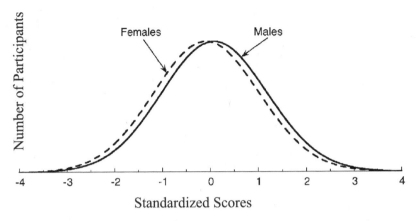

Standardized Scores

From "Gender Differences in Mathematics Performance: A Meta-Analysis," by J. S. Hyde, 1990, *Psychological Bulletin* 107, p. 149.

track specific math abilities. They noted, "based on prior literature. we expected large gender differences to emerge as early as junior high school." It didn't happen. Instead, they found the trajectories of male and female math scores nearly identical all across the age range.[30] (See fig. 3.)

Summers suggested that we need more research to know the truth about girls and math. Not so. There's excellent, sophisticated research that's already been done—which Summers would have known if he had just picked up the phone and called some of the scholars on his own campus. Too many reporters echoed the idea that no good research existed. Sally Quinn, in a column in the *Washington Post,* obviously didn't bother to do her own research when she wrote, "Why don't female mathematicians and scientists, especially at Harvard, get together and research this issue until they have definitive answers instead of reaching for the smelling salts."[31] (Guess what, Sally? They already have.) Writing about that controversy, syndicated columnist George Will said, "There is a vast and growing scientific literature on possible gender differences in cognition. Only hysterics denounce interest in these possible differences . . . as 'bias.'"[32] But is there, indeed, such a "vast literature" finding substantial differences? In fact, the truth is quite the opposite, as Diane Halpern's research, cited above, makes very clear. In the *Washington Post,* Robert J. Samuelson wrote, "many women probably reject science and engineering for another reason: They simply don't find the work

FIG 3. MATH
TRAJECTORIES
FROM AGES 4 TO 18

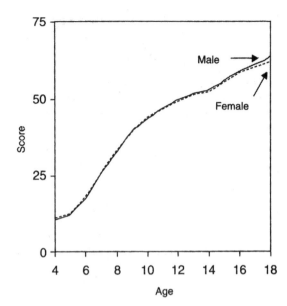

From "Gender
Differences in
Mathematical
Trajectories," by E.
Leahey and G. Guo,
Social Forces 80, pp.
713–32.

appealing, just as they generally don't like football."[33] What's the evidence for this assertion? None. When you examine the facts cited below about the many ways in which girls are discouraged early and often when it comes to math, the idea that women and girls just don't find science and engineering "appealing" seems naïve, at best.

The *Financial Times,* in an editorial, said that Summers launched a "long overdue debate on an issue often judged too sensitive to discuss."[34] But this particular debate has been going on for more than two decades. Many other articles I read simply made the assumption that the issue of gender differences in math had not been studied before and that Summers was to be applauded for "launching new research." Nothing could be farther from the truth, which would have been apparent if some journalists had bothered with adequate research.

Math Aversion

There is a mountain of evidence showing that girls get steered away from math and science at a very early age: Children learn that boys are supposed to be better at math than girls, and the downward spiral begins:

- In the third and fourth grades, boys and girls like math equally. There's no change in fifth and sixth grade for boys, but girls' preference declines. Between the fourth and twelfth grades, the percentage of girls who say they like science decreases from 66 percent to 48 percent.[35]

- In those same years, the percentage of girls who say they would prefer not to study math anymore goes from 9 percent to a whopping 50 percent.[36]
- As grade levels increase, both girls and boys increase their perceptions of math as useful for men. By eighth grade, girls are less likely than boys to enjoy science or math and seem to have less confidence in these subjects.[37]

It's hard to believe it's coincidence or choice that makes girls' enjoyment of math and science dip so severely. Rather, the culture has convinced them that girls don't belong in these fields. And many girls do buy into these ideas—both consciously and unconsciously. The more they accept such ideas, the less likely they are to seriously pursue math careers.

- The power of stereotypes has been documented by the work of psychologist Claude Steele on "stereotype threat." Certain groups— such as African-Americans and women—can suffer an extra burden of anxiety because they are aware of the negative stereotype of the group to which they belong. When they are told that women aren't good at math, women do much worse on a test than when they are told nothing at all before the test. Without the negative information, they score nearly as well as men.[38] (See fig. 4.)

But beliefs about girls' inability in math persist even when the facts say the contrary:

- One 2000 study of third- and fourth-grade children and their parents and teachers found that parents and teachers said they believed that boys were more talented in math—even though the test scores of the actual children showed no gender difference in math.[39]
- In one study of college women majoring in math in 2004, 25 percent believed that males do better at math. Women who held this belief were less likely to go on to grad schools or have math related careers.[40]

Given these facts, you don't have to talk about genes to explain why there aren't more women who seek math careers. And even if it were true that boys *on average* were better at math than girls, there would still be plenty of women out there with the inborn talent to fill high-level posts in academia and industry. Averages mean nothing when it comes to individuals.

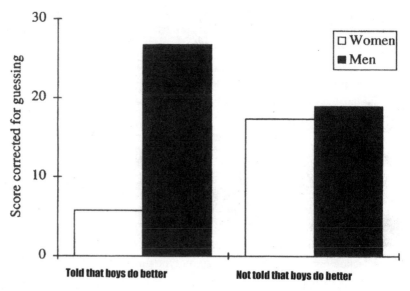

Adapted from "A Threat in the Air: How Sterotypes Shape the Intellectual Identities and Performance of Women and African Americans," by C. M. Steele, 1997, *American Psychologist* 52, pp. 613–29.

Take the case of verbal abilities. On tests that measure mean differences, there are more girls who score at the high end of the ability range than boys. Does that mean that men can't be novelists, editors, screenwriters, poets, political speechwriters, or journalists? Of course not. Does anyone suggest that men are "innately inferior" to females at verbal skills. Not very often. In fact, sophisticated research shows few differences between men and women in this area.

Some argue that the complaints hurled at Summers were just "Political Correctness" and that speech of all kinds should be allowed at universities. But this wasn't just a classroom discussion, it was a statement by the president of Harvard. There is just some speech that is too pernicious (and too wrong) to be uttered by high-level officials. People in such positions should not say that Blacks are dumber than Whites, that Jews are greedier than non-Jews, that Asians are more devious than Caucasians, that Latinos are lazy, that gays are sick and perverse—or that women are inferior to men. Such stereotypes are not supported by science and can do great harm.

But the idea that women aren't naturally good at math has amazing staying power. The math gene controversy I mentioned earlier is a case in point. A team of scientists from Johns Hopkins University examined the math SAT tests of 9,927 gifted seventh and eighth graders. The boys outperformed the girls on the test, which prompted the researchers to draw a startling conclusion. Since the children shared the same classrooms, their experiences must have been the same. Therefore the difference could not be due to environmental factors; it had to be genetic. The researchers suggested that perhaps girls shouldn't even *try* to succeed at math. Their plight was compared to that of a short boy thinking he could make the basketball team.

The influential journal *Science* published the study under the headline "Math and Sex: Are Girls Born with Less Ability?"[41] The mainstream media picked up the cry. The *New York Times* asked, "Are Boys Better at Math?"[42] *Time* looked at "The Gender Factor in Math."[43] The study became a major national story, and many parents worried that their daughters would not be able to compete with their male peers in math. Not long after the first headlines appeared, one of the first talking Barbie dolls burbled, "Math class is hard!" Sadly, some parents even started to look at their daughters differently. That fact was documented by a longitudinal study about ten years later reporting that mothers who knew about the articles lowered their expectations of their daughters' math capabilities.

But critics quickly shot holes in the math gene idea. The researchers had simply assumed that because the boys and girls were in the same classrooms, their experiences were identical. Not so. When another Hopkins scientist interviewed the same group of students, she found that gifted boys' parents picked up on their sons' talents at an early age, bought them math books, and talked with them about their future careers. Gifted girls' parents took little notice of their ability. As I noted above, the pressure on girls to avoid math starts early.

The research mentioned above makes any notion of a "math gene" preposterous. But when the president of Harvard speaks, the media pay attention, even when it's warmed-over nonsense. As biologist Marlene Zuk of UC Riverside told the *Boston Globe,* he had trotted out "the same old lines we've heard for decades—if not for centuries—and they just aren't supported by good data."[44]

And unfortunately, discrimination against women remains. A perfect example of this was a study in which two resumes were sent to college professors to evaluate—sometimes with a male name attached, sometimes a female name. One resume was a "walk-on-water" scholar who had the best of everything. The other was a good but not spectacular scientist, like the resumes that usually come in to academic search committees. Everyone said they'd hire the walk-on-water candidate. But when it came to the good but not spectacular candidate, it was a very different story. When the resume had a male name, wrote Elizabeth Spelke, co-director of the Mind Brain and Behavior Inter-Faculty Initiative at Harvard, the candidate was "rated as having higher research productivity."[45] the scientists

> looked at the same number of publications and thought, "good productivity" when the name was male, and "less good productivity" when the name was female. Same thing for teaching experience. The very same list of courses was seen as good teaching experience when the name was male, and less good teaching experience when the name was female. In answer to the question would they hire the candidate, 70% said yes for the male, 45% for the female. If the decision were made by majority rule, the male would get hired and the female would not.

The professors were asked to express reservations about the good candidates, and tellingly, "those kinds of reservations were expressed *four times more often* when the name was female than when the name was male." And this wasn't just a "guy" thing. Both men and women expressed reservations in a sexist fashion—attesting to the way stereotypes get lodged in our heads even when we don't know they are there.

Just wait. The Harvard flap will die down, no one will talk about a math gene or the inborn ability of girls to do math. (The Summers flap even had a silver lining—a $50 million initiative by Harvard to support initiatives on women scientists and faculty over the next decade.)

Until the next time. Someone will make a remark, cite a flawed study or venture an uninformed opinion. And, once again, the media will resurrect a whole flood of nonscientific nonsense.

11
THE WAR ON BIRTH CONTROL

One of the worst covered stories of the past five years was the Bush administration's war on contraception. The news media barely noticed as the administration put in place the building blocks of a radical agenda to make abstinence the only approved form of preventing birth—here and around the world.

Dr. John D. Miller, director of the Center for Biomedical Communication at Northwestern University's School of Medicine, writes, "Scientists' traditional freedom from bureaucratic interference is being compromised by the Bush administration, which is using appointments to scientific advisory committees as a way to pay off political IOUs to Christian fundamentalist organizations. This has created a dilemma for scientists that they have rarely faced before in the United States."[1]

If you connected the dots, you could have seen that the battle plan was wide-ranging and will have an impact on the health and welfare of millions. But this radical agenda was a nonstory for most of the American media, with brief stories appearing very occasionally on inside pages, the occasional editorial, and steady attention only by a few reporters and columnists.

The debate over stem cells, on the other hand, became a big national story, because not only were possible cures for diseases that affect millions of people involved, but huge bundles of cash for American industries as well. The issues over contraception, most of which were central mainly to women, flew well below the surface of the mainstream media. Checking through Lexis-Nexis, I was surprised to discover how big stories on the issue were more often featured in the British and Canadian media than in the US.

One of the opening salvos in the war was little noticed by the press. On Christmas Eve 2002, in a stealth move, Bush named 11 members to a standing advisory committee of the FDA on reproductive health. None needed Senate confirmation. Among the new appointees were four anti-abortion advocates with a record of opposing reproductive drugs approved by the FDA.[2]

One appointee in particular raised concerns among mainstream scientists. Gynecologist Dr. David Hager helped the Christian Medical Association petition the FDA to reverse its approval of the abortion drug mifepris-tone, which the FDA called safe and effective and approved for prescription use in 1999. Hager objects to oral contraceptives because he says that they provide a "convenient way for young people to be sexually active outside marriage." Hager also wrote a book with his wife that recommends Bible readings and prayers for such ailments as premenstrual syndrome—small relief for millions of women who regularly suffer severe symptoms. Compare the media noncoverage of such outrageous statements with that of Clinton's surgeon general, Joycelyn Elders, who suggested that masturbation would be a good way for teens to experience sexual pleasure without the risk of pregnancy or sexually transmitted diseases. The uproar created by this very sensible suggestion resulted in her firing.

Not surprisingly, David Hager was one of four FDA panel members who voted against making emergency contraceptive pills available over the counter. In 2004, the Bush administration reversed a 23–4 vote in favor of the measure taken by its own FDA panel of scientists. Citing this action, among others, the Union of Concerned Scientists issued a statement signed by a group of researchers that included 48 Nobel Prize winners, 62 National Medal of Science recipients, and 127 members of the prestigious National Academy of Sciences. "The practices we've complained about are still going on," said Cornell University physicist Kurt Gottfried, chairman of the union's board.[3] He said some of the administration's actions reminded him of the Soviet Union's attempts to repress scientists during the Cold War. Despite this, the administration reappointed Hager in 2004.

But the press had barely taken notice of these radical appointees who, some critics say, are decimating US science. Another panelist, Dr. Joseph B. Stanford, refuses to prescribe contraceptives to his patients. These are the people who not only dealt with all women's reproductive health issues, but shaped policy on embryonic stem cell research and on the "personhood" of laboratory fetal tissue.[4]

In 2005, the Food and Drug Administration was under pressure from the medical establishment to make the "morning-after" pill available over the counter for women over 16. After all, it was, said advocates of the drug—including the American Medical Association, the American Academy of Pe-diatrics, and the American College of Obstetricians and Gynecologists—a safe and effective way to reduce the nearly 2 million unwanted pregnancies and hundreds of thousands of abortions in the United States each year. But in an unexpected move, the FDA postponed a decision. Dr. Michael F. Greene, director of maternal fetal medicine at Massachusetts General Hospital, and a member of the FDA's advisory committee, says the agency, "for the first time, appears to be giving in to political pressure."[5] (It was political pressure that finally forced the FDA to approve over-the-counter emergency contraception in 2006. Senators Hillary Clinton and Patty Murray strong-armed Bush by holding up the nomination of his choice for a new FDA commissioner.)

NO MORNING AFTER?

Conservatives have been steadily moving on several fronts to block emergency contraception. The story became a blip in the media for a time, then vanished. In 2004, in Texas, an Eckerd drugstore fired a pharmacist for refusing to sell the legal emergency contraception drug to a rape victim. In Georgia, in 2005, a republican legislator filed a bill requiring that pharmacists who oppose abortion on "moral or religious" grounds and refuse to dispense emergency contraceptive drugs be immune from lawsuits or disciplinary action by employers.[6] Cases where pharmacists refused to sell contraceptives to women or to fill doctors' prescriptions for emergency contraception popped up in California, Washington, Georgia, Illinois, Louisiana, Massachusetts, Texas, New Hampshire, Ohio, and North Carolina. "There are pharmacists who will only give birth control pills to a woman if she's married," reported Adam Sonfield of the New York–based Alan Guttmacher Institute. "There are even cases of pharmacists holding prescriptions hostage, where they won't even transfer it to another pharmacy when time is of the essence."[7]

Even *information* about birth control was targeted by the Bush administration. Twelve House democrats questioned why the National Institutes of Health and the Centers for Disease Control websites removed information about the effectiveness of condoms, replacing it with pro-abstinence propaganda. "Programs That Work," which detailed the success of eight condom-based sex education curriculums, was pulled from the CDC website. Not only that, reports the Council for Research on Women, the new version promoted abstinence only, claiming that condoms could not protect against sexually transmitted diseases. The result of all this could be more unwanted pregnancies and sexually transmitted diseases—and more abortions.[8]

The abstinence-only juggernaut has been a virtual nonstory for most of the American media. Abstinence-only sex education programs for young people aged 9 to 18—69 programs in 25 states—were budgeted in 2004 at $179 million.[9] Indiana state law decrees that schools must "teach abstinence from sexual activity outside of marriage as the expected standard for all school age children"; 20 other states have that legal requirement. In 2006, the Texas Board of Education will begin to use textbooks that advocate traditional marriage and abstinence as the only method for preventing pregnancy and disease. Only 14 out of 50 states require that the subject of contraception be covered at all, and abstinence educators can often only discuss contraception in order to emphasize its limitations.[10]

The press has, overall, failed miserably to report critically on the failures of abstinence-only programs, while the right repeatedly trumpets their successes. In a little-covered press conference in 2005, researchers at the Alan Guttmacher Institute reported that more than 88 percent of adolescents taking "virginity pledges" break them before marriage. Pledges delayed first sex an average of about 18 months for adolescents ages 14 to 16. The really bad news is that teens who take such pledges don't use contraceptives when they do have sex, making them vulnerable to unwanted pregnancies. Pledging teens have the same rate of sexually transmitted diseases as nonpledgers.[11]

In fact, the group Human Rights Watch claimed that, since 1997, the US Congress has allocated more than $350 million—$100 million in fiscal year 2002 alone—to support abstinence-only-until-marriage programs. Such programs, the group says, "deny children basic information that could protect them from HIV/AIDS infection and discriminate against gay and lesbian children. In so doing, these programs not only interfere with fundamental rights to information, to health and to equal protection under the law. They also place children at unnecessary risk of HIV infection and premature death. In the case of HIV/AIDS, what they don't know may kill them."[12]

Parents of children in such programs most likely assume that the information their children do get in such programs is accurate. Not so. A congressional staff analysis found in 2005 that abstinence-only programs gave out "false, misleading, or distorted information."[13] Congressman Henry Waxman pointed out that 80 percent of abstinence-only curricula studied contained false or misleading information. In particular, they blur religion and science; they treat gender stereotypes as scientific fact; and they contain serious scientific errors, such as the notion that abortion leads to sterility and suicide, that pregnancy can result from touching someone's genitals, and that oral sex can give you cancer. As Adrienne Verrilli of the Sexuality Information and Education Council of the United States (SIECUS), notes: "To the Bush administration, science is just an opinion."[14]

This is critical information for parents of teenagers—but they had to search diligently to find it in the US media.

In other actions, the Bush administration ruled that states can make fetuses—instead of pregnant women—eligible for the State Children's Health Insurance Program.[15] Pregnant women would not receive treatment for ailments unrelated to the fetus's needs. For example, excluded completely is all postpartum care, regardless of any complications that might arise during delivery.

A committee designed to protect research subjects was redesigned as a wedge against abortion rights. The Advisory Committee on Human Research Protection has been told to begin to classify embryos as "human subjects." This is an attempt to undermine *Roe v. Wade* by giving new legal rights to embryos. It could also stymie stem cell research that holds promise for diseases such as Parkinson's, diabetes, and Alzheimer's.[16]

Scientific research on human sexuality may fall to ideology. The University of Wisconsin-Madison applied for a $200,000 NIH grant to create a doctoral program in human sexuality research, aimed at bringing more science to the field. But 30 republican legislators asked the Department of Health and Human Services to deny funding, applying the money instead to abstinence-only programs.[17]

INNOCENTS ABROAD?

Most Americans did not vote for a religious-right-based approach to science when they elected Bush, who sold himself as a moderate. But under the cover of the pressing issue of war, an agenda that is far from mainstream forged ahead. In the diplomatic arena, while few in the media paid heed or seemed to care, American foreign policy moved toward opposition to condoms and toward promotion of "natural" birth control methods such as rhythm and abstinence. Under republican presidents, American domestic and foreign policy had been consistently anti-abortion, but usually not overtly against contraception. This changed with George W.—if the country's actions at the Asian and Pacific Conference in Barcelona in 2002 are to be taken as evidence.

The US delegation specifically opposed the use of condoms to block the spread of HIV, one of the fiercest plagues to visit the planet, and urged instead the use of abstinence and the rhythm method.[18] (The latter, we used to say in my parochial school days, was spelled M-O-T-H-E-R-H-O-O-D.)

The US delegation also tried to remove references to adolescents in a section of the report of the conference that dealt with reproductive rights, saying that such a provision would promote sexual activity among teenagers. In Asia, where poor rural girls are lured away from their families by cartels that run huge brothels that advertise underage girls, keeping such girls away from any information about condoms would only fuel the AIDS crisis.

But only the *New York Times* (with a strongly worded editorial), the AP, Knight Ridder (Jodi Enda), and the redoubtable Ellen Goodman seemed to be noticing. A database check several days after the conference found that while coverage in the Asian press was widespread, there was little coverage in the American press of a major conference that seemed to have moved this nation to a position of opposition to all forms of contraception except abstinence and rhythm.

While 32 nations voted for the plan that reaffirmed the reproductive rights of women and girls, the US alone voted against such provisions. Nasreen Pervin Hug[19] of the Helen Keller International Group in Bangladesh told the South China *Morning Post:* "The U.S. is trying to impose ideologies. It seems perfectly willing to give U.S. women certain rights, but not to recognize the extension of those rights to others."

By 2004, little had changed. At a Bangkok conference, the Bush administration was still arguing that condoms promote promiscuity, while AIDS experts from around the world call the US position dangerous. "In an age where 5 million people are newly infected each year and women and girls too often do not have the choice to abstain, an abstinence-until-marriage program is not only irresponsible, it's really inhumane," US Congresswoman Barbara Lee (D-California) said.[20]

At home, Bush put Christian conservatives in charge of fighting AIDS and instructing the nation's youth in matters of sex. Claude Allen, a former top aide to Jesse Helms, went to HHS as deputy health secretary, where he was a strong advocate of abstinence-only sex education. Former congressman (now senator) Tom Coburn of Oklahoma was appointed co-chair of the presidential Advisory Council on HIV and AIDS. Coburn is a vociferous opponent of using condoms to prevent AIDS. As executive director of the group, Bush appointed Patricia Funderburk Ware, who advocated the idea that abstinence until marriage is the proper formula for sexual conduct. (She was forced to retire when one of her appointees, a Christian conservative, disclosed he had made slurring remarks about gays.)[21]

"Compassionate Conservatism," it seems, means that death is preferable to sex, for teenagers or by anyone who is not married. It apparently means that condoms are a greater danger to the women of the world than AIDS, even though the UN says that in Africa alone, half of the 4 million new cases of AIDS are among females. Planned Parenthood's Gloria Feldt says that the administration's war on choice has as its first victims the most vulnerable: women and children and their families in developing nations.[22]

The news media not only seriously underplayed this crucial issue, but did the same on a massive pro-choice march (organizers say more than a million people attended) in Washington in the spring of 2004. The website Womensenews noted that editors didn't think there was going to be a big turnout, and gave the march little advance billing.[23] When the march turned out to be one of the biggest gatherings ever, the group Fairness and Accuracy in Reporting (FAIR) monitored the coverage, and noticed that the women's march got much less coverage than a march by the conservative Christian men's group, The Promise Keepers, in 1997.[24]

The three major networks aired a combined total of six stories on the march. Cable coverage of the event wasn't much better. MSNBC did not cover the event, while CNN ran several stories throughout the day on Sunday but aired "just a small handful" of brief stories before and after the event. The three largest newsweeklies virtually ignored the event, according to a Lexis-Nexis search conducted by Womensenews. Of the three largest newsmagazines, *Newsweek* was the only one to cover it at all. The magazine ran a piece in the back of the book in its April 26 edition that highlighted ambivalence toward abortion rights on the part of young women. The story did not mention the surprisingly high turnout of young people at the demonstration. *Time* and *U.S. News and World Report* passed over the event altogether.

BANNING BIRTH CONTROL

While the political assault on contraception continued unabated, there were ominous signs that the next assault in the war against birth control would be an attempt to remove from the market any substance—including the pill and the IUD—that might have even the *possibility* of affecting fertilization. In Wisconsin, pro-lifers have backed legislation that would ban any medicine or drug that has any intent "other than to increase the probability of a live birth." Pro-Life Wisconsin's website makes it clear the group wants to ban "the I.U.D., Depo-Provera, Norplant and other chemical combinations being used . . . [T]his also includes all forms of the birth control pill currently being sold."[25] The group calls "sinful" all types of contraception except abstinence. Bills have been crafted in that state and others to write that notion into law. Check out a range of pro-life websites and you will find declarations that all forms of contraception except the rhythm method are, in fact, abortion-causing agents because they cause changes in the lining of the uterus that might prevent a fertilized egg from implantation. Pro-Life Tennessee defines a "single cell" as a human life.

All these initiatives against contraception, says Rachel Laser of the National Women's Law Center in Washington, are "outrageous." She sees the real issue as sex discrimination. "It prevents access to a basic form of health care for women. We're going back in time."[26]

It is literally mind-blowing to see that the news media for all intents and purposes ignored the war on contraception—one of the major stories of the era. (Not until the spring of 2006 did the *New York Times Magazine* weigh in with a cover article, an excellent—if belated—treatment of the issue.) It was a story that involved life and death, global politics, the control of birth, and the AIDS plague—and one that will have an impact on virtually every man, woman, and child on the planet. "It is a jeremiad against women who want to control every facet of their destiny. The campaign against sex education, against condoms—and now against a tiny pill that sits in the medicine chests of millions of American homes—is a comprehensive assault on modern life," wrote *Newsday* columnist Marie Coco."[27]

That women's reproductive health is largely in the hands of religious conservatives opposed even to contraception seems unthinkable more than 40 years after the Supreme Court struck down laws against birth control. This sinister fact has implications for every woman in America. And yet, it was a story that was nearly invisible to the gatekeepers of the American media.

BLAME THE PILL

While the Bush administration waged war on birth control on religious grounds, historian Francis Fukuyama argued that the pill caused illegitimacy, divorce, single-parent families, poverty, crime, poor education, and drug use.

In his 1999 book on social trends, *The Great Disruption: Human Nature and the Reconstitution of Social Order,* Fukuyama focused on the dire consequences of women controlling their own reproduction.[28] Once again, it's all women's fault. When women step out of traditional roles, chaos descends. (The argument has a long history; for example, critics decreed that giving women the vote would produce social upheaval, marriages would shatter, and children would suffer.)

Fukuyama became one of those "celebrity academics" when he had a 1992 bestseller with *The End of History.* So *The Great Disruption* was widely reviewed in the mass media, often favorably. Fukuyama seems to love everything about global capitalism except the fact that women get a share of the goodies. Unfortunately, when academics become celebrities, they tend to get a great deal of media attention, even when their theories are routinely questioned by other scholars.

Fukuyama argues that, in the early 1960s, society enforced strict rules on young men who impregnated their girlfriends, forcing them to marry the girls. Twenty years later, he argues, the pill had "liberated men rather than women from the responsibility for the children they created." The fatherless households that subsequently emerged, he says, contributed to social ills such as poverty, crime, poor education, and drug use. He says that in Japan, where health officials have recently approved the pill, chaos will soon descend. He argues that Asian societies are more crime free because women don't work.

Where does one even start to dispute this strange version of Western society? This argument mistakes correlation for causation. One might argue that the introduction of the pill was associated with a time of freer sexuality, but pill users were *not* the ones having lots of babies. The explosion of unwed motherhood associated with social chaos was centered mainly in the underclass, which was also plagued by a crack-cocaine epidemic. One could say, in fact, that *not* using the pill was the cause of drugs and illegitimacy, since middle- and upper-class college kids on the pill were not having babies or using crack. In fact, poor men had traditionally felt free to sire children and desert them, because they lacked the resources to support them. The pill had little impact on illegitimacy in poor neighborhoods.

The free sexuality that emerged in the 1960s in the middle class was due to demographics, because probably never before in the history of the country were so many people young at the same time—thanks to the Baby Boom. But after they outgrew "sex, drugs and rock and roll," boomers settled down and on the whole became productive adults. Middle-class boomers did not end up mugging people on the streets or killing each other over drugs.

Fukuyama says that violent crime declined in Japan and Korea during a period (late sixties through early nineties) in which crime increased in the United States and Europe. But tying the pill and women's employment to an increase in crime makes no sense. In the mid and late 1990s in the United States, as women's employment rate soared, with over half of the mothers of toddlers in the US work force, crime plunged dramatically. Does this mean that working mothers *decrease* crime? Of course not. The two are most likely not related. A drop in the number of young men, better policing, and tougher sentences during this period accounted for the statistics.

In the United States, where use of the pill is widespread and lots of women work, homicide rates are high. In Scandinavia, where female employment is very high and birth control nearly universal, homicide rates are low. Clearly, homicide rates have no connection to birth control, one way or the other.

As for the low crime rates in Japan, it is a country with a homogenous population, strong cultural traditions of respect for authority, and a great deal of peer pressure. Whether Japanese women have the pill or not has little impact on overall criminality.

In the United States, it's absurd to say that women's control over reproduction is the cause of social disruptions, when deindustrialization and the loss of high-paying industrial jobs is reshaping the economy, creating an urban underclass with no way out. Add racial tensions, increased mobility, worries about security, and the shrinking of the middle class. In fact, one could argue that the pill helped to reduce the instability brought about by deindustrialization. Male wages have been stagnant or declining for 30 years; what has kept middle-class families from dropping into poverty is the wages of working women. The decreased fertility of these women, and their incomes, kept families afloat, so one could argue for the pill as a strong stabilizing force.

Fukuyama speaks favorably of Japan, where "male resources were exchanged for female fertility." But could the forced dependence and the isolation of women such a policy produced be one reason for Japan's dismal economy? Many bright Japanese women who study in the United States stay here rather than return home, where they see few opportunities. An emerging phenomenon in Japan is "marriage strikes," where women choose good jobs over the restrictions of traditional marriage. At any rate, Fukuyama's model is an artifact of the past. Statistics say that women's lives are going to extend into their nineties. Keeping women out of the labor force and dependent on shrinking male wages is a recipe for disaster. Control of fertility allows women to support themselves and avoid widespread penury.

The pill may avoid social chaos in another way. On a fragile planet, where resources are feeling the weight of human numbers, we must control population. There is no need to restrict women only to childbearing when too many children are the problem for the earth. And if birth rates are declining in the developed world, immigration assures a supply of young workers. The United States offers a good example of how this can work. Unlike some other societies, where immigrants are never accepted as "real" citizens, new arrivals to America are often assimilated quickly—especially if they are young and not dirt-poor. They wear Nikes and baseball caps, know the lyrics to rap songs, and pick up the slang. Already, in the United States, we are seeing more marriages among white, brown, and black young people. Only those wedded to white supremacy see this as tragic. In my own family, for example, I have a grandson and granddaughter who are part Filipino and a new grand-nephew who is part Salvadoran. I think it's wonderful.

But the pull of traditional roles and of the inherent "rightness" of male supremacy remains strong. Equality is just fine for everybody except women. And ever since Eve, women have been blamed for the loss of paradise. The news media too often mindlessly agree. It's a hard habit of mind to shake.

CONCLUSION AGAINST FORGETTING

The story about the truth matters more than the truth itself. Journalists used to believe they were simply collecting bits of reality, solid as rock. As Sergeant Friday used to say on *Dragnet,* "Just the facts, ma'am." That is far too simplistic a notion. As sociologist William Gameson notes, "Facts have no intrinsic meaning; they take on their meaning by being embedded in a frame or story line that organizes them and gives them coherence, selecting certain ones to emphasize while ignoring others."[1]

Another favorite saying in journalism classes is that reporters hold up a mirror to reality, reflecting back simply what is there. Media scholars no longer believe that to be true. As critic Todd Gitlin writes, the news media are "far from mirrors passively reflecting reality." The facts that journalists report are indeed out there in the real world, but are "out there *among others.*" The media reflection is not reality, but the "active, patterned, remaking performed by mirrors in the fun house."[2]

The fun house mirror of the news media serves women ill in several ways: first, by creating storylines that do not reflect the reality of the lives of the majority of women, and also by projecting a distorted image of both historical and present-day feminism—the vehicle though which women's rights were advanced and secured.

The narratives that so appeal to the marketing culture of the media and that sell anxiety to women readers, as we've seen, get endlessly recycled. Social science data repeatedly debunk ideas such as *women will be unhappy if they seek good jobs,* or *men won't marry smart women,* but such notions persist because they sell. Anxiety is as marketable as lipstick. And, in the age of the Internet, immortal as well.

The anti-feminist bias in the media is unmistakable. Proof of this comes from a 2002 study of the major electronic media by Rebecca Ann Lind of the University of Minnesota and Colleen Sato of the University of Illinois, Chicago.[3] They surveyed 35,000 hours of ABC, CNN, PBS, and NPR news and public affairs programming and discovered that feminists were portrayed differently than "regular" women. "First of all, feminists appear rarely and are often demonized. The most common words attached to feminists were 'radical, militant, raging, and masculine.' Feminists were ten times more likely to be associated with words such as jerks, bitches, radical or bad than were 'regular' women."

While feminists were less often presented as victims than ordinary women, they were presented as being quite different from most women. As the researchers noted, "Feminists are odd. If audiences reflect the media's framing of feminists and women, we should not be surprised if future research discovers that people believe something like 'feminists don't do the same types of things that regular women do, and there aren't that many of "them" out there anyway.' Such a perspective does not encourage people to embrace feminist goals and ideals; indeed it may well do just the opposite."

This anti-feminist media storyline combines with a major narrative of American history, identified by Alexis de Tocqueville: individualism. In his classic *Democracy in America* (1835), de Tocqueville worried that when Americans "have acquired or retained sufficient education and fortune to satisfy their own wants . . . they acquire the habit of always considering themselves as standing alone, and they are apt to imagine that their whole destiny is in their own hands."[4]

This illusion, de Tocqueville notes, "throws [the American] back forever upon himself alone and threatens in the end to confine him entirely within the solitude of his own heart."

The rugged individualism that de Tocqueville saw in the seventeenth century has today morphed today into what I call "hyper-individualism." Society and its success, its failures, its trends and its history are seen as the product of individual people making individual decisions, based on their own moral virtue—or lack of it. And virtue is too often defined as how much stuff you have. As historian Robert McElvaine notes, consumption has replaced work as the central, valued activity of people's lives. "Descartes has been modified. Now the disconnected person seeking assurance of being says: *I consume, therefore I am.*"[5]

As conservative, individualist ideas saturate the news media, it becomes harder to examine the consequences of a market economy or to solve social problems in a community-centered way. After all, we do not inhabit a Jeffersonian system of hardy yeoman farmers. We live in a 24-7, incredibly fast-paced technological society, where citizens are more and more interconnected with each other. However, the news media buy into individualized ways of thinking about social and familial issues, and as a result, promote paralysis. In other areas of our life, we are quite comfortable with innovative ways of solving problems. The mid-level manager who takes part in creative "brainstorming" teams and task forces during the day at work comes home to struggle with child care on her own—just as every other woman on the block is doing. Hyper-individualism makes it difficult, if not impossible, to design systems for the problems families face in real time. Many of our institutions are structured as if it were still 1950 (or 1850). Why do schools get out at 3 pm? So kids can go home and help their parents pick crops and feed and water the animals. Our education timetable hasn't yet outgrown the agricultural age, much less entered the post-industrial age.

The anti-feminist and the hyper-individualist media frames wind around each other in troublesome ways. This might be unimportant if the move to secure women's rights had been accomplished. But as many scholars have noted, the revolution is only half complete, even though enormous gains have indeed been made. In the nineteen fifties and sixties, when I was coming of age, a woman's fate depended entirely on the man she would marry. The only white collar jobs routinely open to women were low-paid ones— teacher, secretary, nurse. (And even then, a woman was apt to be fired if she got pregnant.) Virtually no high-paid, prestigious jobs were available to women.

My female students today find that unimaginable. But they also underestimate the roadblocks they will face once they get into the workforce, where the majority of them will spend most of their lives. My students and their children, if they have them, may have a lifespan of nearly a century. By some estimates, a healthy baby girl born today has a one in three chance of reaching age 90. Many of her friends will live to see the twenty-second century. Marshall Carter, chairman and CEO of the State Street Corporation, says, "We jokingly say that this new baby girl's first words shouldn't be "Mama" or "Dada"—they should be "long-term, growth-oriented investment strategy."[6]

Yet the news media encourage women to focus on the increasingly small segment of their lives when they will be raising young children. Today, most women will spend more time with their children as adults than as children, and will have to support themselves for very long lives. Still, popular media narratives applaud women for deciding to become housewives while they are in college, and later, if they do have good jobs, for deserting them to care for aging parents on the "daughter" track.

In fact, "care" is perhaps the most urgent issue in the American domestic arena. It affects the lives of every one of us, male or female, young or old. Who will care for young children, for aging adults, for the many people who are now alive because of our modern medicine but need assistance? The performance of a news media increasingly obsessed with infotainment and trivia, forsaking serious social science while spinning anti-feminist narratives, inhibits the development of policies to meet this urgent need. Storylines such as the selfish mother, the menace of day care, the threat of ambition, and the notion that only women are designed to care and nurture, offer no answers in a world where the majority of women are spending most of their lives in the workforce and most couples are on the job. Professor Jody Heymann, of McGill University, founder of the Global Working Families Project at the Harvard School of Public Health, says,

As we enter the twenty-first century, the picture in the United States is clear. Women do significantly more of the household chores (78 percent of women report that women carry more of this burden, as do 85 percent of men). Women are more likely than men to provide care for children, elderly parents, disabled adults, and children with disabilities or special needs. While women bear more of the caregiving burden, they face worse working conditions than men. They are less likely to have sick leave, vacation leave, or to have any flexibility in the workplace. Moreover, a majority of the pay gap between women and men is associated with their differing family responsibilities.[7]

The search for high-quality day care is the number one stressor of working couples, male or female, making it clearly an issue that is central to the American economy.[8] Yet the coverage of the child care issue skews toward bogus scare stories about "bullies." The failure of the news media to make work-family issues a high priority is one of the reasons for the dismal American record in this critical area. Consider these startling facts from Harvard's Global Working Families project:[9]

- 37 countries guarantee parents some type of paid leave when children fall ill. The US does not.
- 163 countries offer paid maternity leave. The US does not.
- All industrialized countries except Australia offer paid family and medical leave. The US does not. And Australia guarantees a full year of unpaid leave while the US offers 12 weeks.
- 45 countries offer paternity leave. The US does not.
- 76 countries protect working women's right to breastfeed. The US does not.
- 96 countries mandate paid annual leave. The US does not.

- 84 countries limit the maximum work week employers can require. The US has no limit on mandatory work.
- 40 countries have mandated evening and night wage premiums. The US does not.
- The US is tied for 39th with Ecuador and Surinam for enrollment in early childhood education for 3–5 year olds.
- The US is tied for 91st out of 151 countries in preprimary student to staff ratios.

Why do the American media believe it is front page news when a few Ivy League female students say they want to be housewives, and invent bogus "mommy wars," while generally ignoring a huge national crisis right before their eyes?

It is common knowledge that most families hang onto a middle-class lifestyle only because they have two incomes. As Nicholas Kulish wrote in an op ed in the *New York Times,* "These days, Ward Cleaver wouldn't be able to afford a house in the suburbs or Beaver's tuition unless June went to work. No version of the American dream is cheap."[10] The cost of raising a child, he notes, is estimated at $217,000, not including college tuition.

The struggle of American families should be a major narrative of our time, but editors mostly yawn. At the Work-Family-Journalism conference in Boston in 2004, many journalists complained that they could simply get no interest from editors on stories about how other nations solved problems of day care, elder care, health issues, retirement, vacation time, overtime, etc.

We know that media storylines affect the way Americans look at reality. When the patterning of the fun house mirror comes into play, reality shifts into peculiar shapes. Take the "selfish mother" storyline, for example. As I noted earlier, mountains of evidence show that working women and their children are doing well, and there is virtually no difference between the children of women at home and women at work on any measure of social and cognitive development. Still, in 2003, NYU sociologist Kathleen Gerson reported that 48 percent of Americans believe that preschoolers suffer if their mothers work, and 42 percent of employed parents themselves thought that working mothers care more about succeeding at work than meeting their children's needs.[11]

Editors and reporters carry these distorted ideas around in their heads, along with the rest of us, and it shows on the printed page or in the electronic sound bite. The result? People feel guilty about making the right choices for their families, both economically and for the well-being of themselves and their children. They buy the anxiety the media is selling. Kathleen Gerson says, "The challenge facing us is not whether good workers can also be good mothers, but whether we can create the conditions that enable working mothers and fathers to be good parents."[12]

One of the great supports I had facing the work-family struggle was a feminist movement that gave me legitimacy, the sense that I was not alone, and the idea that women could indeed band together to make political change. Like me, *Chicago Parent* editor Susy Schultz spent years struggling with being both a parent and a worker, and now sees younger women facing exactly the same struggle—with *fewer* supports than we had.[13] Anti-feminist narratives undercut women's ability to see the issues in their personal lives as political issues, which is the key first step to political action. Schultz says, "As I see it, we have but one choice and that is to build a strong coalition that supports parents, although it is akin to turning around a 747—particularly in this climate. And it's just hard to find the time. Most of us are changing diapers—sometimes those of our kids and sometimes those of our parents."

An anti-feminist narrative makes it less likely that young women will be able to wage effective political action on issues like sexual harassment in the workplace, sex discrimination, domestic violence, wage differentials, the dearth of family-friendly policies at work, the "second shift" at home, the erosion of reproductive rights, and a whole range of issues that still bedevil society. The idea that feminism is dead, that women have enough rights— too many, in fact, and should not ask for more—is the subtext of many news stories (such as the "war on boys").

The media's eternal search for the "new" is a factor in all this—but, in fact, anti-feminism is now an old story. As Patricia Bradley points out in *Mass Media and the Shaping of American Feminism, 1963–1975,* a full-blown backlash against feminism set in as early as the late seventies, and "mass media's pursuit of the new, counter-feminist messages came to replace feminism on the news agenda and helped set in place the conservative revolution of the 1980s."[14]

Or, as *Times* columnist Maureen Dowd complained, "Maybe we should have known that the story of women's progress would be more of a zigzag than a superhighway, that the triumph of feminism would last a nanosecond while the backlash lasted 40 years."[15]

Too often, media images help to convince educated young women that the "movement" that made possible the lives of accomplishment that they now expect was composed of a bunch of bra-burning man-haters. (Just as, when I was growing up, my image of "Suffragettes" was that of crazy ladies chaining themselves to buildings. Women's history has a way of morphing into caricatures of loony females.)

When one young woman, 24-year-old Alison Stein,[16] now an official at the National Council of Women's Organizations, was in college at the University of Pennsylvania, she roomed with liberal women who were active in groups such as College Democrats. But when she asked them to join her in a pro-choice group or at the university women's center, they told her they agreed with her ideas but that they weren't feminists.

"I said if these women aren't feminists, then who are feminists?" said Stein.

Who, indeed?

To my students, and to other young women who may worry about asking for too much, stepping over too many boundaries, being disliked, turning into "feminazis," I would repeat the words of Gloria Steinem. She once said, "I have met brave women who are exploring the outer edge of human possibility, with no history to guide them and with a courage to make themselves vulnerable that I find moving beyond words."[17]

That journey through the galaxies of possibility is still an ongoing one for women. Now at least, we do have history to guide us—even though the news media at times seem bent on obliterating it. We must grasp that history and hold on hard—lest we forget what we have learned about courage and risk, and about the need to dream.

NOTES

INTRODUCTION (I – 14)

1. World Health Organization, "50 Facts," www.who.int/whr/1997/media_centre/50facts/en/index.

2. Pete Hamil, *News Is a Verb: Journalism at the End of the Century* (New York: Ballantine Publishing Group, 1998).

3. Howard Kurtz, "The All-Boy Network: Public Affairs Shows Reflect Shortage of Women in Power," *Washington Post,* December 5, 2001.

4. "News Networks Overlooking Women Experts," *Women's Funding Network,* October 11, 2005, www.wfnet.org/pressroom/viewnews.php?story_id=286.

5. E. Noelle Neumann, *The Spiral of Silence: Public Opinion—Our Social Skin* (Chicago: University of Chicago Press, 1993).

6. "A Feminist Timeline," Department of Women's Studies, Ohio State University website: http://womens-studies.osu.edu.

7. Spiro Agnew, "Spiro T. Agnew Quotes," www.brainyquote.com.

8. Gina Bellafante, "Is Feminism Dead?" *Time,* June 20, 1998.

9. Stephanie Coontz, *Marriage, a History: From Obedience to Intimacy* (New York: Viking, 2005).

10. Michele Conlin, "The New Gender Gap: From Kindergarten to Grad School, Boys Are Becoming the Second Sex," *Business Week,* May 26, 2003.

11. Richard B. Freeman, "The Feminization of Work in the United States: A New Era for (Man)Kind," in Siv Gustaffson and Daniele Meulders, eds., *Gender and the Labor Market: Econometric Evidence on Obstacles in Achieving Gender Equality* (New York: Macmillan, 2000).

12. Barbara Ehrenreich and Deirdre English, *For Her Own Good* (New York: Anchor Doubleday, 1979).

13. Stephanie Coontz, *The Way We Never Were: American Families and the Nostalgia Trap* (New York: Basic Books, 1992); Arlene Skolnick, *Embattled Paradise: The American Family in an Age of Uncertainty* (New York: Basic Books, 1991); Steven Mintz and Susan Kellog, *Domestic Revolution: A Social History of American Family Life* (New York: Free Press, 1988).

14. Michael Lind, "Right and Wrong," *Boston Globe,* January 13, 2003.

15. George Will, "Damned Lies and . . . ," *Newsweek,* March 29, 1999.

16. Barbara Ehrenreich and Deirdre English, "Witches, Midwives and Nurses, a History of Women Helpers," tmh.floonet.net/articles/witches.html.

17. M. F. Belenky, B. M. Clinchy, N. R. Goldberger, and J. M. Tarule, *Women's Ways of Knowing: The Development of Self, Voice, and Mind* (New York: Basic Books, 1986).

I. SUPERWOMEN AND TWITCHING WRECKS (PP. 15 – 23)

1. "The Lies Parents Tell About Work, Kids, Day Care and Ambition," *US News,* May 12, 1997.

2. Laura Shapiro, "The Myth of Quality Time," *Newsweek,* May 12, 1997.

3. "The Majority of Working Women Are Stressed Out," *UPI,* March 27 1991.

4. "Female Managers Face Super Stress," *Chicago Tribune,* May 8, 1989.

5. "Working Women Stressed Out," Reuters, March 27, 1991.

6. "Life's a Nightmare for Today's Middle-Class Working Mothers," *The Guardian,* August 10, 2002.

7. "A Blues Epidemic," *Business Week,* September 26, 1988.

8. "Are You Headed for Overload?" *Redbook,* June 1990.

9. Rosalind C. Barnett and Caryl Rivers, *She Works/He Works: How Two Income Families Are Happier, Healthier, and Better Off* (San Francisco: Harper, 1996).

10. Elaine Wethington and Ronald Kessler, "Employment, Parental Responsibility and Psychological Distress," *Journal of Family Issues,* December 1989.

11. Grace Baruch, Rosalind Barnett, and Caryl Rivers, *Lifeprints: New Patterns of Love and Work for Today's Women* (New York: McGraw-Hill, 1983).

12. "Working Women Fare Better," *Boston Globe* (wire dispatch), September 17, 1995.

13. Susanna Haynes, "Work, Women and Coronary Heart Disease," *American Journal of Public Health* 70 (1980).

14. Wethington and Kessler, "Employment . . ."

15. Aletha C. Huston and Stacey Rosenkrantz Aronson, "Mothers' Time with Infant: Quality, Not Quantity, Most Important in Early Infant Development," summarized from *Child Development,* 6:2, Society for Research in Child Development, March 25, 2005.

16. Jeff Melnick, "Letters," *Boston Globe,* November 1, 2004.

17. Barbara Ehrenreich, *Nickel and Dimed: On (Not) Getting By in America* (New York: Metropolitan, May 2001).

18. "More Supermoms Are Hanging Up Their Capes," *Orlando Sentinel,* April 22, 1994.

19. "Is Superwoman Shedding Her Cape?" *Atlanta Constitution,* May 2, 1994.

20. "The Failed Superwoman," *Ebony,* May 1994.

21. "Superwoman Has Had Enough," *The Independent,* June 20, 1994.

22. Alex Kuczyński, "They Conquered, They Left," *New York Times,* March 24, 2002.

23. Lisa Belkin, "The Opt-Out Revolution," *New York Times Magazine,* October 26, 2003.

24. Kathleen Gerson, "Working Moms Heading Home? Not Likely," Listserv, Council on Contemporary Families, CCF@ listserv.unh.edu.

25. Heather Boushy, "Are Mothers Really Leaving the Workplace?" Council on Contemporary Families website, March 28, 2006, www.contemporaryfamilies.org.

26. Rochelle Sharpe, "As Leaders, Women Rule," *Business Week,* November 20, 2000.

27. Linda K. Stroh, Jeanne M. Brett, and Anne H. Reilly, "All the Right Stuff: A Comparison of Female and Male Managers' Career Progression," *Journal of Applied Psychology,* 77:3 (1992).

28. Richard Abelson, "If Wall Street Is a Dead End, Do Women Stay to Fight or Go Quietly?" *New York Times,* August 3, 1999.

29. Ibid.

30. Louise Story, "Many Women at Elite Colleges Set Career Path to Motherhood," *New York Times,* September 20, 2005.

31. Jack Shafer, "A Trend So Old It's New," *Slate,* September 25, 2005.

32. Katha Pollitt, "Desperate Housewives of the Ivy League," *The Nation,* June 19, 2006.

33. Radcliffe Public Policy Center, *Life's Work: Generational Attitudes Towards Work and Life Integration* (Cambridge: Radcliffe Center for Advanced Study, 2000).

34. Gerson, "Working Moms . . ."

35. "HHS Issues Report Showing Dramatic Improvements in America's Health Over Past 50 Years," National Center for Health Statistics, September 12, 2002, www.hhs.gov.

36. Teresa and H. John Heinz III Foundation, The Women's Retirement Initiative, http://www.hfp.heinz.org/programs/.

2. TOO TIRED FOR SEX, TOO LATE FOR BABIES? (PP. 24 – 34)

1. Editorial, "They're Too Smart for These Guys," *Chicago Sun Times,* December 15, 2005.

2. "Are Men Insecure or Are They Merely Intimidated?" *Toronto Star,* January 7, 2005.

3. John Schwartz, "Glass Ceilings at Altar as Well as Boardroom," *New York Times,* December 14, 2004.

4. Maureen Dowd, "Men Just Want Mommy," *New York Times,* January 13, 2005.

5. Maureen Dowd, "What's a Modern Girl to Do?" *New York Times Magazine,* October 30, 2005.

6. Stephanie Brown and Brian Lewis, "Relational Dominance and Mate-Selection Criteria: Evidence that Males Attend to Female Dominance," *Evolution and Human Behavior* 25 (2004).

7. Valerie K. Oppenheimer, "Women's Employment and the Gain to Power: The Specialization and Trading Model," *Annual Review of Sociology* 23 (1997).

8. Heather Boushey, "Baby Panic Book Skews Data," Womensenews, August 30, 2002.

9. Stacy J. Rogers and D. D. DeBoer, "Changes in Wives' Income: Effects on Marital Happiness, Psychological Well Being and the Risk of Divorce," *Journal of Marriage and Family* 63, (2001).

10. Alice Eagly and Wendy Wood, "The Origins of Sex Differences in Human Behavior: Evolved Dispositions Versus Social Roles," *American Psychologist* 54 (1999).

11. M. D. Taylor, C. L. Hart, G. Davey Smith, L. J. Whalley, D. J. Hole, V. Wilson, and I. J. Deary, "Childhood IQ and Marriage by Mid-life: The Scottish Mental Survey 1932 and the Midspan Studies," *Personality and Individual Differences* 38 (2005).

12. "Too Smart to Marry?" *Atlantic,* April 2005.

13. Dowd, "What's a Modern Girl to Do?"

14. Eloise Salholz, "The Marriage Crunch," *Newsweek,* June 2, 1986.

15. "Are These Women Old Maids?" *People Magazine,* March 31, 1986.

16. Eloise Salholz, The "Marriage Crunch."

17. Daniel McGinn, "Marriage by the Numbers," *Newsweek,* June 5, 2000.

18. Allison Pearson, *I Don't Know How She Does It* (New York: Knopf, 2002).

19. Roxanne Roberts, "The Whole Mom Catalogue," *Washington Post,* November 12, 2002.

20. Ralph Gardner, Jr., "Who's the Better Mom?*" New York Magazine,* October 21, 2002.

21. Caitlin Flanagan, "The Wifely Duty," *Atlantic Monthly,* February 2003.

22. Abigail Stewart, "Role Combination and Psychological Health in Women," paper presented at the meeting of the Eastern Psychological Association, 1978.

23. Janet. S. Hyde, John D. DeLamater, and E. E. Hewitt, "Sexuality and the Dual-Earner Couple: Multiple Roles and Sexual Functioning," *Journal of Family Psychology,* 12 (1998).

24. Rosalind Chait Barnett and Caryl Rivers, "The 'Epidemic' of Childlessness," *Boston Globe,* April 27, 2002.

25. Ilana DeBare, "A Female Success Story: More Businesses Than Ever Owned by Women in U.S." (*San Francisco Chronicle*), Center for Women's Business Research website, www.womensbusinessresearch.org/mediacenter; Ronald Kotulak, "Increase in Women Doctors Changing the Face of Medicine," *Chicago Tribune,* January 12, 2005; "Women Physicians—Good News and Bad News," *New England Journal of Medicine,* 334:15 (April 11, 1996).

26. David Dunson et al, "Changes with Age in the Level and Duration of Fertility in the Menstrual Cycle," *Human Reproduction,* 17:5 (May 2002).

27. Emma Ross, "Running Out the Clock," *Montreal Gazette,* April 30, 2002.

28. Maureen Freely, "Sorry, Too Late," *London Independent,* April 19, 2002.

29. Nick Tate, "Don't Let Window of Fertility Slip Away," *Atlanta Journal Constitution,* April 16, 2003.

30. Diana Griego Erwin, "Waiting Longer for Babies May Mean Not Having Them at All," *Sacramento Bee,* April 14, 2002.

31. Nancy Gibbs, "Babies vs. Career," *Time,* April 15, 2002.

32. Sylvia Ann Hewlett, *Creating a Life: Professional Women and the Quest for Children* (New York: Talk Miramax, 2002).

33. Janice M. Horowitz, "Second Opinions," *Time,* December 30–January 6, 2003.

34. Dowd, "What's a Modern Girl to Do?"

35. Warren St. John, "The Talk of the Book World Still Can't Sell," *New York Times,* May 20, 2002.

36. Boushey, "Baby Panic . . ."

37. Ibid.

38. Grace Baruch, Rosalind Barnett, and Caryl Rivers, *Lifeprints: New Patterns of Love and Work for Today's Women* (New York: McGraw-Hill 1983).

39. Ibid.

40. Katha Pollitt, "Backlash Babies," *The Nation,* May 13, 2002.

3. DIVORCE AND DISRUPTION (PP. 35 – 41)

1. Judith Wallerstein, "Children After Divorce," *New York Times Magazine*, January 22, 1989.

2. Barbara Dafoe Whitehead, "Dan Quayle Was Right," *The Atlantic*, April 1993.

3. Judith Wallerstein (with Julia Lewis and Sandra Blakeslee), *The Unexpected Legacy of Divorce* (New York: Hyperion, September 2000). Also, Judith Wallerstein and Sandra Blakeslee, *Second Chances: Men, Women and Children a Decade After Divorce* (New York: Simon and Schuster, 1991).

4. Margaret Talbot, "No Joy In Splitsville," *New York Times Book Review*, October 1, 2000.

5. Elisabeth Lasch-Quinn, "Loving and Leaving: The Pursuit of Unhappiness in America," *New Republic*, May 6, 2000.

6. Constance Ahrons, *We're Still Family* (New York: Harper Collins, 2004).

7. Mavis Hetherington and John Kelly, *For Better or For Worse: Divorce Reconsidered* (New York: Norton, 2002).

8. Frank Furstenberg and Andrew J. Cherlin, *Divided Families: What Happens to Children When Parents Part?* (Cambridge, Mass.: Harvard University Press, 1991).

9. Kathy Boccella, "Book Spurs Divorce Debate," *Philadelphia Inquirer*, March 31, 2002.

10. Paul R. Amato, Laura Spencer, Alan Booth, "Parental Divorce, Marital Conflict and Offspring Well Being During Early Adulthood," *Social Forces* 73:3 (March 1989).

11. Abigail Stewart, Anne Copeland, Nia Lane Chester, Janet Malley, and Nicole Barenbaum, *Separating Together: How Divorce Transforms Families* (New York: Guilford 1997).

12. Nicholas Wolfinger, "Beyond the Intergenerational Transmission of Divorce," *Journal of Family Issues* 21:8 (November 2000).

13. Andrew Cherlin et al., "Longitudinal Studies on Effects of Divorce on Children in the United States and Great Britain," *Science*, June 7, 1991.

14. "Study Disputes Divorce as Cause of Child's Problems," *Los Angeles Times*, June 7, 1991.

15. Hetherington and Kelly, *For Better or For Worse* . . .

16. James Q. Wilson, *The Marriage Problem: How Our Culture Has Weakened Families* (New York: Harper Collins, 2002).

17. Stephanie Coontz, *The Way We Never Were: American Families and the Nostalgia Trap* (New York: Basic, 1992).

18. Michael Ignatieff, "Liberalism vs. Family Values," *Toronto Star*, January 22, 1998.

4. SUFFER THE LITTLE CHILDREN (PP. 42 – 54)

1. Editorial, "The Nanny Verdict: Backlash," *St. Louis Post Dispatch*, November 3, 1997.

2. William Safire, "Trusting a Stranger," *New York Times*, November 9, 1997.

3. Michael Kelly, "A Heedless Bias Against Parents," *Boston Globe*, January 15, 1998.

4. Stephanie Coontz, *The Way We Never Were: American Families and the Nostalgia Trap* (New York: Basic Books, 1992); Arlene Skolnick, *Embattled Paradise: The Ameri-*

can *Family in an Age of Uncertainty* (New York: Basic Books, 1991); Steven Mintz and Susan Kellog, *Domestic Revolution: A Social History of American Family Life* (New York: Free Press, 1988).

5. Lois Hoffman, "Effects of Maternal Employment in the Two-Parent Family," *American Psychologist*, 1989.

6. Marcia Guttentag, "Women, Men and Mental Health," in L. Cater, A. Scott, and W. Martyna, eds., *Women and Men: Changing Roles* (Aspen Institute for Humanistic Studies, 1975); also see Frederick Ilfeld, Jr, "Sex Differences in Psychiatric Symptomology," paper delivered to the American Psychological Association, 1977; Jessie Bernard, *The Future of Marriage* (New York: World Times, 1972).

7. NICHD Early Child Care Research Network, "The Effects of Infant Child Care on Infant-Mother Attachment Security: Results of the NICHD Study of Early Child Care," *Child Development* 68 (1997).

8. Penelope Leach, *Children First* (New York: Knopf, 1994).

9. Gwen Kinkead, "Spock, Brazelton and Now . . . Penelope Leach," *New York Times Magazine*, April 10, 1994.

10. NICHD Early Child Care Research Network, "The Effects of Infant Child Care . . ."

11. Robert C. Pianta, "Grant Allows U. Va. Curry School to Continue Study of Children as Part of Large-Scale National Effort," University of Virgina News, www.virginia.edu, February 4, 2000.

12. Kathleen Parker, "Connecting the Dots Between Day Care and Bullies," *Denver Post*, April 25, 2001.

13. "Day Care Turns Out Bullies," wire services, *Ottawa Citizen*, April 20, 2001.

14. Philip Cowan, CCF@listserv.unh.edu, June 15, 2001.

15. Jay Belsky and J. M. Braungart, "Are Insecure-Avoidant Infants with Extensive Day-Care Experience Less Stressed by and More Independent in the Strange Situations?" *Child Development* 62 (1991). See also Robert Karan, "Becoming Attached," *Atlantic Monthly*, February 1990.

16. John Bowlby, *Maternal Care and Mental Health* (New York: Shocken, 1951).

17. Bruno Bettelheim, *The Children of the Dream* (New York: Macmillan, 1969).

18. Philip Wylie, *Generation of Vipers* (New York: Holt Reinhart and Winston, 1955).

19. Margaret Talbot, "The Disconnected," *New York Times Magazine*, May 24, 1998.

20. Arlie Russell Hochschild, *The Time Bind: When Work Becomes Home and Home Becomes Work* (New York: Metropolitan Books, 1997).

21. Laura Shapiro, "The Myth of Quality Time," *Newsweek*, May 1997.

22. Todd Gitlin, *Media Unlimited: How the Torrent of Images and Sounds Overwhelms Our Lives* (New York: Metropolitan Books, 2002).

5. THE MOMMY DIARIES (PP. 55 – 66)

1. Susan J. Douglas and Meredith W. Michaels, *The Mommy Myth* (New York: Free Press, 2004).

2. Ibid.

3. Jason De Parle, *American Dream: Three Women, Ten Kids, and a Nation's Drive to End Welfare* (New York: Viking, 2004).

4. Douglas and Michaels, *The Mommy Myth.*

5. Ibid.

6. Ibid.

7. Betty Burton, "Selfish Parents Need to Grow Up," *Atlanta Journal and Constitution,* September 15, 1999.

8. "Selfish Parents Just Won't Sacrifice for Kids," *Chicago Sun Times,* July 7, 2002.

9. Stephanie Coontz, *The Way We Never Were: American Families and the Nostalgia Trap* (New York: Basic Books, 1992).

10. Ibid.

11. Steven Mintz and Susan Kellog, *Domestic Revolution: A Social History of American Family Life* (New York: Free Press, 1988).

12. Coontz, *The Way We Never Were.*

13. Laurel Thatcher Ulrich, *A Midwife's Tale: The Life of Martha Ballard, Based on Her Diary 1785–1812* (New York: Vintage, 1990).

14. Tamar Lewin, "Now a Majority: Families with Two Parents Who Work," *New York Times,* October 24, 2000.

15. Mintz and Kellog, *Domestic Revolution.*

16. John F. Sandberg and Sandra L. Hofferth, "Children's Time with Parents," US, 1981–1997, *Demography* 38 (3).

17. Suzanne M Bianchi, Lynne M. Casper, and Rosalind B. King, eds., *Work, Family, Health and Well-Being* (Mahwah, N.J.: Lawrence Erlbaum Associates, 2005).

18. "Felicity Huffman Has Arrived," *CBS News, 60 Minutes,* www.cbsnews.com/stories/2006/01/12/60minutes/main1203852page3.shtml.

19. Mona Gable, "Is Lesley Stahl a Good Mother?" *Huffington Post,* www.huffingtonpost.com/mona-gable/is-lesley-stahl-a-good-mob14050.html.

20. Jane Gross, "Forget the Career. My Parents Need Me at Home," *New York Times,* November 24, 2005.

21. "Revisiting the Mommy Wars," *Christian Science Monitor,* May 30, 2001.

22. Edward Wyatt, "New Salvo Is Fired in Mommy Wars," *New York Times,* November 2, 2004.

23. Ralph Gardner, Jr., "Who's the Better Mom?" *New York Magazine,* October 21, 2002.

24. "Mommy Wars Incited by Irresponsible Media, Says NOW President Kim Gandy," *Media Report to Women* 34:2 (Spring 2006).

25. Alan Wolfe, *One Nation, After All: How the Middle Class Really Think About God, Country, and Family* (New York: Viking Press, 1998).

26. Stephanie Coontz, "To Work or Not to Work," *Christian Science Monitor,* July 21, 1998.

27. Deirdre D. Johnson and Debra Swanson, "Invisible Mothers: A Content Analysis of Motherhood Ideologies and Myths in Magazines," *Sex Roles,* July 2003.

28. Claudia Wallis, "The Case for Staying Home," *Time,* March 22, 2004.

29. Kelly Knauer, *Time A to Z Health Guide* (New York: Time Books, 2004).

30. Daphne de Marneffe, *Maternal Desire: On Children, Love and the Inner Life* (New York: Warner Books, 2006).

31. Judith Warner, *Perfect Madness: Motherhood in the Age of Anxiety* (New York: Riverhead, 2005).

6. THE MUTED VOICE (PP. 67 – 74)

1. James Rainey, "A Very Public Opinion Exchange," *Los Angeles Times,* March 11, 2005.

2. Howard Kurtz, "LA Woman (vs. LA Man)," *Washington Post,* March 7, 2005.

3. Alicia Mundy, "The Pack Rat," *Editor and Publisher,* November 25, 2002.

4. Kurtz, "LA Woman . . ."

5. Mundy, "The Pack Rat."

6. Geneva Overholser, "Women with a Strong Point of View," *Washington Post,* December 7, 2000.

7. Katha Pollitt, "Invisible Women," *The Nation,* April 4, 2005.

8. Ibid.

9. Carol Slezak, "Masters at Silencing a Voice," *Chicago Sun Times,* April 10, 2005.

10. James T. Madore, "Women's Views Absent in the News," *Newsday,* May 23, 2005.

11. Ina Howard, "On Party, Gender, Race and Class, TV News Looks to the Most Powerful Groups," *Extra!,* May-June 2002.

12. "News Networks Overlooking Women Experts," *Women's Funding Network* 10/11/05, www.wfnet.org/pressroom/viewnews.php?story_id=286.

13. Ruth Davis Konigsberg, "Ratio of Male to Female Writers in National 'General Interest' Magazines," WomenTK.com.

14. Jennifer Weiss, "The Gentleman's Club," *Columbia Journalism Review,* July-August 2005.

15. Carl Swanson, "Brainy Young Things," *New York Magazine,* April 10, 2006.

16. Sandra Tsing Loh, "Uber-Mom Overload," *Atlantic,* June 2005.

17. *Atlantic,* June 2006.

18. Christina Hoff Sommers, *The War Against Boys: How Misguided Feminism Is Harming Our Young Men* (New York: Simon and Schuster, 2000).

19. Caitlin Flanagan, "Dispatches from the Nanny Wars: How Serfdom Saved the Women's Movement," *Atlantic,* March 2004.

20. Christina Nehring, "Latex Conquers All," *Atlantic,* October 2005.

21. Boston Women's Health Book Collective, *Our Bodies, Ourselves* (New York: Simon and Schuster, 2005).

22. Benjamin Wittes, "Letting Go of Roe," *Atlantic,* January/February 2005.

23. Dennis Loy Johnson, "The Talk of the Rest of the Town," July 29, 2002, Moby-Lives, http://mobylives.com/NYer_survey.html.

24. Paula Caplan and Mary Ann Palko, "The Times Is Not a-Changing," *Women's Review of Books,* November 2004.

25. American Press Institute and the Pew Center for Civic Journalism, www.newspaper.org, July 18, 2004.

26. Mary Arnold, Marlene Lozada Hendrickson, and Cynthia C. Linton, "Women in Newspapers: 2003," The Media Management Center at Northwestern, www.mediamanagementcenter.org/center/web/publications/win2003.htm.

27. "News Staffs Shrinking While Minority Presence Grows," American Society of Newspaper Editors, April 12, 2005, www.asne.org.

28. Michele Weldon, "No News in Newsroom Census: Gender Gap Persists," Womensenews, April 21, 2004.

29. American Society of Newspaper Editors, April 12, 2005.

30. Nancy Cook Lauer, "Studies Show Women's Role in Media Shrinking," Womensenews, May 21, 2002.

31. Sheila Gibbons, "Inequities Persist for Women in Media," Womensenews, January 21, 2004.

32. Ibid.

33. Howard Kurtz, "The All-Boy Network: Public Affairs Shows Reflect Shortage of Women in Power," *Washington Post,* December 5, 2001.

34. Sheila Gibbons, "Newspaper Execs Clueless about What Women Want," womensenews, September 17, 2003.

35. Peter Edmonston, "At Forbes.com, Lots of Glitter, Not So Many Visitors," *New York Times,* August 28, 2006.

7. HATING HILLARY (PP. 75 – 84)

1. Dan Kennedy, "The Trouble with Being Hillary," *Boston Phoenix,* June 17–23, 2005.

2. John Podhoretz, *Can She Be Stopped? Hillary Clinton Will Be the Next President of the United States Unless . . .* (New York: Random House, 2006).

3. Edward Klein, *The Truth about Hillary: What She Knew, When She Knew It and How Far She'll Go to Become President* (New York: Sentinel, 2005).

4. "Rage at Author After Claim: Bill Raped Hillary, Conceived Chelsea," June 2005, http://www.drudgereport.com/flash3ek.htm.

5. "Klein Backs Off Rape Smear in Hannity Interview Meltdown," *Media Matters for America,* mediamatters.org, June 22, 2005.

6. Tina Brown, "Hillary Clinton Attacked by Man from Mars," *Washington Post,* June 23, 2005.

7. Edward Wyatt, "Biography of Senator Clinton Has a Few Unexpected Critics," *New York Times,* June 24, 2005.

8. Dick Polman, "A New Mission for Sen. Clinton's Antagonists," *Philadelphia Inquirer,* June 19, 2005.

9. Katherine Corcoran, "Pilloried Clinton," *Washington Journalism Review,* January-February 1993.

10. Hillary Rodham Clinton, *Living History* (New York: Simon and Schuster, 2004).

11. Lloyd Grove, "The Ungagable Teresa Heinz," *The Washington Post,* May 6, 2003.

12. Jennifer Foote, "Who's Afraid of Teresa Heinz," *Salon,* May 14, 2003.

13. Joan Vennochi, "'The Teresa' Shows Us The Power of Money," *Boston Globe,* May 15, 2003.

14. Melinda Henneberger, "Loose Cannon—Or Crazy Like a Fox?" *Newsweek,* May 3, 2004.

15. John Tierney, "Speaking Her Mind, Using Her Checkbook," *New York Times,* May 13, 2003.

16. Maureen Dowd, "Breck Girl Takes On Dr. No," *New York Times,* July 8, 2004.

17. Richard Halicks, "Politics 2004: Winners and Losers: Familiar Faces, Some of Which We May Rarely See Again," *Atlanta Journal-Constitution,* January 2, 2005.

18. David Rennie, "Money to Burn—and a Mouth to Fan the Flames," *London Telegraph,* November 4, 2004.

19. Collin Levey, "Putting a Lid on the Loose Lips of Teresa Heinz Kerry," *Seattle Times,* July 29, 2004.

20. Marshall McLuhan, *The Medium is the Message* (Cambridge Mass.: MIT Press, 1998).

21. Joan Vennochi, "Unelectable Frontrunner?" *Boston Globe,* August 7, 2003.

22. White House Project, www.barbaraleefoundation.org/.

23. "Keys to the Governors Office," www.barbaraleefoundation.org/.

24. Caroline Heldman, Susan J. Carroll, and Stephanie Olson, "Gender Differences in Print Media Coverage of Presidential Candidates: Elizabeth Dole's Bid for the Republican Nomination," paper prepared for delivery, American Political Science Association, August 31/September 3, 2000.

25. Patricia Sellers, "Power; Do Women Really Want it?" *Fortune,* October 13, 2003.

26. Harvey Mansfield, *Manliness* (New York: Yale University Press, 2006).

27. Chronicle News Services, "Bork Goes Before Appeals Panel in Seeking New Trial for Helmsley," *Houston Chronicle,* October 24, 1992.

28. "Rhymes with Rich," *Newsweek,* August 1989.

29. Marco R. Della Cava, "Has Stewart Changed Her Stripes?" *USA Today,* March 28, 2005.

30. "Martha's Last Laugh," *Newsweek,* March 7, 2005.

31. "Disgraced Hotel Queen Set for Jail," *The Advertiser* (Associated Press), April 16, 1992.

8. LADIES OF THE RIGHT (PP. 85 – 97)

1. David Carr, "Deadly Intent: Ann Coulter, Word Warrior," *New York Times,* June 12, 2006.

2. Ann Coulter, *Godless: The Church of Liberalism* (New York: Random House, 2006).

3. Adam Lisberg, "Massive Chip on Her Coulter," *New York Daily News,* June 6, 2006.

4. Carr, "Deadly Intent."

5. Ann Coulter, *Treason, Liberal Treachery from the Cold War to the War on Terrorism* (New York, Random House, 2004).

6. John Cloud, "Is She Serious or Just Having Fun?" *Time,* April 25, 2005.

7. "Ann Coulter Quotes," brainyquote.com.

8. "Time Covers Coulter," *Action Alert,* Fair.org website, April 21, 2005.

9. Ann Coulter, *Slander: Liberal Lies about the American Right* (New York: Crown, 2002).

10. Kate O'Beirne, *Women Who Make the World Worse: How Their Radical Feminist Assault Is Ruining Our Schools, Families, Military, and Sports* (New York: Sentinel, 2006).

11. Christina Hoff Sommers, *Who Stole Feminism: How Women Have Betrayed Women* (New York: Simon and Schuster, 1995).

12. "Independent Women's Forum," Sourcewatch, the Center for Media and Democracy, www.sourcewatch.org.

13. Danielle Crittenden, *What Our Mothers Didn't Tell Us: Why Happiness Eludes the Modern Woman* (New York: Simon and Schuster, 1999).

14. Christina Hoff Sommers, *The War Against Boys: How Misguided Feminism Is Harming Our Young Men* (New York: Simon and Schuster, 2000).

15. Peg Tyre; with Andrew Murr, Vanessa Juarez, Anne Underwood, Karen Springen, and Pat Winget, "The Trouble with Boys: They're Kinetic, Maddening and Failing at School. Now Educators are Trying New Ways to Help Them Succeed," *Newsweek,* January 30, 2006.

16. Michael Kimmel, "What about the Boys?" *WEEA Digest* (Newton, Mass.: Women's Educational Equity Act Resource Center, November 2000).

17. Ibid.

18. Richard Whitmire, "Boy Trouble," *New Republic,* January 23, 2006.

19. Valerie Lee and Anthony Bryk, "Effects of Single-Sex Secondary Schools on Student Achievement and Attitudes," *Journal of Educational Psychology* 78 (1986).

20. Jay Mathews, "Study Casts Doubt on the 'Boy Crisis,'" *Washington Post,* June 26, 2006.

21. Caryl Rivers and Rosalind Chait Barnett, "The Myth of the Boy Crisis," *Washington Post,* April 9, 2006.

22. Ibid.

23. Peg Tyre et. al., "The Trouble with Boys."

24. Michele Conlin, "The New Gender Gap: From Kindergarten to Grad School, Boys Are Becoming the Second Sex," *Business Week,* May 26, 2003.

25. Rivers and Barnett, "The Myth of the Boy Crisis."

26. Christina Hoff Sommers, *The War Against Boys, Atlantic,* May 2000.

27. Ibid.

28. American Association of University Women, "Shortchanging Girls, Shortchanging America," Full Data Report, Washington, DC, 1990.

29. Jacqueline E. Woods, "Don't Blame Girls, Women," *USA Today,* August 29, 2003.

30. Marabel Morgan, *Total Woman* (New York: Revell, 1974).

31. Laura Doyle, *The Surrendered Wife: A Practical Guide to Finding Intimacy, Passion, and Peace with Your Man* (New York: Simon and Schuster, 2001).

32. Laura Schlessinger, *The Proper Care and Feeding of Husbands* (New York: Harper Collins, 2004).

33. Caryl Rivers, *Aphrodite at Midcentury: Growing Up Female and Catholic in Mid-century America* (New York: Doubleday, 1974).

34. Jessie Bernard, *The Future of Marriage* (New York: World Times, 1972).

35. John Harlow, "Anti-Feminist Wife," *Toronto Star,* January 27, 2001.

36. Andrea Dworkin, *Right Wing Women: The Politics of Domesticated Females* (New York: Perigee, 1983).

37. Genevieve Antoine Dariaux, *The Men in Your Life: Timeless Advice and Wisdom on Managing the Opposite Sex* (New York: Morrow, 2005).

9. NEWS AS POLI-PORN (PP. 98 – 108)

1. Steven Mintz, *Huck's Raft: A History of American Childhood* (Cambridge Mass.: Belnap Harvard, 2004).

2. Elena Gaona, "Disappearances along Border Spur Activism: Missing Women Focus of Program," *San Diego Union-Tribune,* March 23, 2005.

3. Jessica Heslam, "Media Frenzy Absent in this Brutal Story," *Boston Herald,* May 5, 2006.

4. Ibid.

5. Alex Tresniowski, Siobhan Morrissey, Elizabeth Cobb, Inez Russell, Michael Haederle, Deborah Geering, Lori Johnson, Aaron Baca, Steve Helling, Natasha Stoynoff, K.C. Baker, "Runaway Bride," *People Magazine,* May 16, 2005.

6. Susan Sontag, "The Double Standard of Aging," *Saturday Review of Literature* 39 (1972).

7. Robin Givhan. "The Eyelashes Have It," *Washington Post,* November 18, 2000.

8. Hayley Kaufman, "Fashion Victim," *Boston Globe,* November 16, 2000.

9. Monica Collins, "From Chads to Egads, Florida Fiasco Rivals O.J. Trial," *Boston Herald,* November 16, 2000.

10. "Monroe vs. Hurley" (short), *Chicago Sun-Times,* May 30, 2001.

11. Clara Jeffrey, "Limited Ambition," Mother Jones website, www.motherjones.com/neos//exhibit/2006/01/limited_ambitions.

12. Robin Gerbner, "Why Turn Brilliant Lawyer into Barbie with Brains?" James MacGregor Burns Academy of Leadership, www.academy.umd.edu.

13. Margery Eagan, "What a Surprise: Harris Draws Catty Comments," *Boston Herald,* November 16, 2000.

10. BRAINPOWER (PP. 109 – 124)

1. Michael Gurian, "Disappearing Act," *Washington Post,* December 4, 2005.

2. Michael Gurian, *The Wonder of Girls: Understanding the Hidden Nature of Our Daughters* (New York: Pocket Books, 2002).

3. Gail Swainson, "Girls Not Wired for Science, Author Claims," *Toronto Star,* January 10, 2002.

4. Andrew Herrmann, "Girls, It Seems, Will be Girls," *Chicago Tribune,* February 17, 2002.

5. K. C. Kling, J. S. Hyde, C. J. Showers, and B. N. Buswell, "Gender Differences in Self-esteem: A Meta-analysis," *Psychological Bulletin* 125:4 (1999).

6. *Library Journal,* September 15, 1996.

7. Valerie Strauss, "Educators Differ on Why Boys Lag in Reading: Gap Stokes Debate Over Teaching Approaches, Curricula," *Washington Post,* March 15, 2005.

8. Diane F. Halpern, *Sex Differences in Cognitive Abilities* (Mahwah N.J.: Erlbaum, 2000).

9. Stephen Jay Gould, *The Mismeasure of Man* (New York: W. W. Norton, 1996).

10. April Austin, "Is It a Girl's Nature to Nurture?" *Christian Science Monitor,* February 27, 2002.

11. Carol Tavris, *The Mismeasure of Woman* (New York: Touchstone, Simon and Schuster, 1992).

12. Anne Moir and David Jessel, *Brain Sex: The Real Difference Between Men and Women* (New York: Viking, 1997).

13. Simon Baron-Cohen, *The Essential Difference: The Truth about the Male and Female Brain* (New York: Basic Books, 2003).

14. Ibid.

15. Dr. Amir Raz, "Mail Call," *Newsweek,* September 22, 2003.

16. Simon Baron-Cohen, "The Male Condition," *New York Times,* August 8, 2005.

17. Sandy Starr, "Life Lessons: What Is the One Thing Everyone Should Learn about Science?" *The Guardian,* April 7, 2005.

18. Maria Kubacki, "Nature or Nurture: How Science Has Helped Us Discover that Boys Will Be Boys and Girls Will Be Girls," *Ottawa Citizen,* March 19, 2005.

19. Sarah Baxter, "Mars, Venus Still Gender Benders," *Weekend Australian,* February 12, 2005.

20. Emma Crichton-Miller, "The Gender's Not for Bending: Men and Women Have Different Kinds of Biological Brains After All," *London Telegraph,* May 4, 2003,

21. "The Difference Between Boys and Girls," *Parents,* March 2006; also "Born to Build?" September 2003.

22. Elizabeth Spelke, "Sex Differences in Intrinsic Aptitude for Mathematics and Science, a Critical Review," *American Psychologist,* December 2005. Also "The Science of Gender and Science, Pinker vs. Spelke, a Debate," Edge, the third culture website, Harvard University Mind/Brain/Behavior initiative, Edge:www.edge.org/3.

23. Ibid.

24. S. Connor, "Men Aren't Heartless—It's All in the Mind," *The Independent (London),* July 23, 2002.

25. Michelle Conlin, "The New Gender Gap: From Kindergarten to Grad School, Boys Are Becoming the Second Sex," *Business Week,* May 26, 2003).

26. Faye Crosby, *Juggling: The Unexpected Advantages of Balancing Career and Home for Women* (New York: MacMillan, 1991).

27. Brent Bridgeman and Cathy Wendler, "Gender Differences in Predictors of College Mathematics Performance and in College Mathematics Course Grades," *Journal of Educational Psychology,* 83:2 (1991).

28. J. S. Hyde, E. Fennema, and S. J. Lamon, "Gender Differences in Mathematics Performance: A Meta Analysis," *Psychological Bulletin,* 107:2 (1990).

29. Diane F. Halpern, *Sex Differences in Cognitive Abilities* (Mahwah, N.J.: Erlbaum, 2000).

30. Erin Leahey and Guang Guo, "Gender Differences in Mathematical Trajectories," *Social Forces* 80 (2001).

31. Sally Quinn, "The Misguided Mathematics of Equating Women and Men," *Washington Post,* February 19, 2005.

32. George Will, "Harvard Hysterics," *Washington Post,* January 27, 2005.

33. Robert J. Samuelson, "Sanctioned Silences," *Washington Post,* January 26, 2005.

34. "Summerstime Blues" (editorial), *Financial Times,* February 9, 2005.

35. S. L. Boswell, "The Influence of Sex-Role Stereotyping on Women's Attitudes and Achievement in Mathematics," in S. F. Chipman, L. R. Brush, and D. M. Wilson, eds., *Women and Mathematics: Balancing the Equation* (Mahwah, N.J.: Erlbaum, 1985), 91.

36. Ibid.

37. Ibid.

38. Claude M. Steele, "A Threat in the Air: How Stereotypes Shape the Identities and Performance of Women and African Americans," *American Psychologist* 52 (1997).

39. Rosalind C. Barnett and Caryl Rivers, "New Gender Myths Supported by Dubious Research," July 20, 2005, Brandeis.edu/news.

40. Ibid.

41. Camilla P. Benbow and Julian C. Stanley, "Math and Sex: Are Girls Born with Less Ability?" *Science* 210 (1980).

42. "Are Boys Better at Math?" *New York Times,* December 7, 1980.

43. "The Gender Factor in Math," *Time,* December 15, 1980.

44. Deborah Blum, "Solving for XX," *Boston Globe,* January 23, 2005.

45. Spelke, "Sex Differences . . ."

II. THE WAR ON BIRTH CONTROL (PP. 125 – 134)

1. Caryl Rivers, "In Age of AIDS, Condom Wars Take Deadly Toll," www.womensenews.org, December 10, 2003.

2. Michael Lasalandra, "Bush Appointee Blasted over Prayer-for-PMS Advice," *Boston Herald,* October 28, 2002.

3. David Kohn, "Researchers Renew Criticism of Bush Administration: Prize-Winners Say Politics Overshadows Science," *Baltimore Sun,* July 9, 2004.

4. Gina Kolata, "Debate on Selling Morning-After Pill Over the Counter," *New York Times,* December 12, 2003.

5. Susan Baer, " 'Morning After' Pill: Still Delayed by FDA," *Baltimore Sun,* January 30, 2005.

6. Carlos Campos, "Legislature '05: Abortion Foes Target Use of Pill; Druggists May Refuse to Dispense," *Atlanta Journal-Constitution,* February 4, 2005.

7. Rob Stein, "Pharmacists' Rights at Front Of New Debate: Because of Beliefs, Some Refuse to Fill Birth Control Prescriptions," *Washington Post,* March 28, 2005.

8. Letter to Tommy G. Thompson from Henry Waxman et al, *Congressional Record,* Washington, December 18, 2002.

9. Barbara Miner, "A Look Ahead, with Concern about Reproductive Rights," *Milwaukee Journal Sentinel,* June 22, 2003.

10. "Abortion Anxiety Mounts in U.S," *Toronto Star,* January 29, 2005.

11. Gaby Wood, "Worth the Wait?: Conservative America Is Extending the Politics of Fear—Into the Bedroom," *The Observer,* February 6, 2005. Also, Marina Pisano, "Studies Challenge Abstinence-Only: Researchers Share Their Results on Teen Sex at News Briefing," *San Antonio Express-News,* January 21, 2005.

12. "Bush Policies Hurt AIDS Prevention, Groups Say: Administration Accused of Disinformation on Condom Use," *Washington Post,* October 1, 2002.

13. "Abortion Anxiety Mounts in U.S," *Toronto Star,* January 29, 2005.

14. Wood, "Worth the Wait?"

15. William Saletan, "What's the Value of a Fetus?" *New York Times,* October 26, 2003.

16. "Advisory Panel: What Protections for Children, Fetuses, Embryos?" Alliance for Human Research Protection, www.ahrp.org/infomail/1002/30.php.

17. "University of Wisconsin-Madison Seeking Funding for Human Sexuality Doctorate Program," www.siecus.org.

18. "Seeing Beyond Roe, Bush Aims at Contraception," www.womensradio.com/reallife/Health/bush_contraceptive.htm.

19. Asia Source, www.ASIASOURCE.org.

20. Vijay Joshi, "Condoms Are the Weapon of Choice: Bush's Abstinence Policy Seen as Setback in AIDS Battle," *Montreal Gazette,* July 13, 2004.

21. "AIDS Panel Director Leaves Amid Controversy Over Activist," *Washington Post,* February 5, 2003.

22. Gloria Feldt, *The War on Choice: The Right-Wing Attack on Women's Rights,* April 13 2004, www.plannedparenthood.org/pp2/portal/media/pressreleases/pr-040413-feldt-book.xml

23. Allison Stevens, "Media Play Was Light for Rally's Heavy Turnout," Womensenews, May 6, 2004.

24. "Women's March Coverage Hard to Find on Television News": Fairness and Accuracy in Reporting, http://www.fair.org/activism/womens-march-networks.html.

25. "Forcing Birth Control Coverage Is Forcing Abortion Coverage," www.prolifewisconsin.org, August 18, 2004.

26. Stein, "Pharmacists' Rights . . ."

27. Marie Cocco, "A Senator Enables a Retreat to the Past," *Newsday,* November 23, 2004.

28. Francis Fukuyama, *The Great Disruption: Human Nature and the Reconstitution of Social Order* (New York: Free Press, 1999).

CONCLUSION (PP. 135 – 141)

1. William Gamson and Andre Modigiani, "Media Discourse and Public Opinion on Nuclear Power," *American Journal of Sociology* 95 (1989).

2. Todd Gitlin, *The Whole World Is Watching: Mass Media in the Making and Unmaking of the New Left* (Berkeley Calif.: University of California Press, 1980).

3. Rebecca Ann Lind and Colleen Sato, "The Framing of Feminists and Feminism in News and Public Affairs Programs in U.S. Electronic Media," *Journal of Communication,* March 2002.

4. Alexis de Tocqueville, *Democracy in America* (1835; New York: Signet Classic, September 2001).

5. Robert McElvaine, *Eve's Seed: Biology, the Sexes, and the Course of History* (New York: McGraw Hill, 2001).

6. Marshall N. Carter, "The Aging of the World's Population and Its Impact on Asia: Risks and Rewards," Asia Society—CEO Forum Series, New York, February 1, 2000, www.asiasociety.org/speeches/carter.html.

7. Boston Review, "Jody Heymann Replies," February-March 2002, www.bostonreview.net/BR27.1/heymann2.html.

8. Rosalind C. Barnett and Caryl Rivers, *She Works/He Works: How Two Income Families Are Happier, Healthier, and Better Off* (San Francisco: Harper, 1996).

9. "The Work, Family, and Equity Index: Where Does the United States Stand Globally? U.S. Lags Far Behind Most Countries in Ensuring Decent Conditions That Allow Workers to Care for Children and Family," *Global Working Families Project, Harvard School of Public Health,* www.hsph.harvard.edu/globalworkingfamilies/.

10. Nicholas Kulish, "Changing the Rules for the Team Sport of Breadwinning," *New York Times,* September 23, 2005.

11. Kathleen Gerson, "Work Without Worry," Council on Contemporary Families website (reprinted from the *New York Times,* May 11, 2003), www.contemporaryfamilies.org.

12. Ibid.

13. Susy Schultz, private communication, June 22, 2006.

14. Patricia Bradley, *Mass Media and the Shaping of American Feminism, 1963–1975* (Jackson, Miss.: University Press of Mississippi, 2003).

15. Maureen Dowd, "What's a Modern Girl to Do?" *New York Times Magazine,* October 30, 2005.

16. Mary Lynn F. Jones, "Young Women Meet in D.C., Create Own Movement," *Womensenews,* February 3, 2005.

17. Gloria Steinem, "Gloria Steinem quotes," About Education website, Women's History, http://womenshistory.about.com/cs/quotes/a/qu_g_steinem.htm.

INDEX